Owney, the Post Office Dog
and Other Great Dog Stories

Compiled and Edited by Joe L. Wheeler

Pacific Press® Publishing Association

Nampa, Idaho

Oshawa, Ontario, Canada

www.pacificpress.com

Cover art by: Lars Justinen

Designed by: Justinen Creative Group

Interior illustrations from the library of Joe L. Wheeler

Copyright © 2004
Pacific Press® Publishing Association
Printed in United States of America

Additional copies of this book are available
by calling toll free 1-800-765-6955 or
by visiting http://www.adventistbookcenter.com

Library of Congress Cataloging-in-Publication Data

Owney the post-office dog and other great dog stories/[edited by] Joe L. Wheeler.
p. cm.–(The good Lord made them all)
ISBN: 0-8163-2045-4
1. Dogs–United States–Anecdotes. I. Wheeler, Joe L., 1936- II. Series

SF426.2.O96 2004

636.7–dc22   2004054282

04 05 06 07 08 · 5 4 3 2 1

Dedication:

To Pinto

My brother Romayne lives on the rim of Mexico's Copper Canyon (which is deeper and broader than the Grand Canyon of the Colorado). Some time ago, a visitor asked my brother if he could have Pinto, saying, "Since you have four other dogs, you don't really need him. Well, *I do!*" So my brother reluctantly parted with Pinto, and the dog was taken to a place far from the rim. Ten days later, what should appear but Pinto, lame and with bleeding feet. Somehow, some way, he had found his way home through 110 miles of the most rugged and inaccessible terrain and the deepest canyon in North America. And only that once had Pinto ever been away from home!

Pinto recently breathed his last breath—but it was there on the canyon rim and by the master he so loved.

CONTENTS

Introduction - Only the Dog
Joseph Leininger Wheeler and Albert Payson Terhune

Owney, the Post Office Dog - *Joseph Leininger Wheeler* 12

The Tail of the Lobo - *Penny Porter* 26

The Inhumanities - *Julia Tavenner M'Garvey* 31

The Killer - *Verne Athanas* 42

Wolf - *Albert Payson Terhune* 58

Delayed Delivery - *Cathy Miller* 74

His Adopted Friend - *Abbie Farwell Brown* 80

Scottie Scores a Triumph - *John Scott Douglas* 89

It Isn't Done - *M. F. Simmonds* 96

When Tad Remembered - *Minnie Leona Upton* 104

Captain Kidd's Ribbons - *Dee Dunsing* 113

Annie, the Railroad Dog - *Phil Walker* 120

To Everything a Season - *P. J. Platz* 124

Don - *Zane Grey* 137

Introduction:
Only the Dog

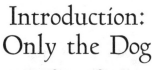

Joseph Leininger Wheeler
(with Albert Payson Terhune)

Just think about it: Down through recorded history, which species, of all species of wildlife, has always remained inseparable from the human? Not the horse; it roams free when it has the chance. Not cows, goats, chickens, or sheep—none of them *live* with us. Not even the cat. Even though millions of them have lived with humans for thousands of years, always the cat has done so on its own terms, continuing to maintain its independence. That leaves only the dog to have unreservedly cast its lot with men, women, and children. To a cat, we may represent a part of its life; to a dog, we represent *all* of its life.

In literature, the first starring role for a dog was in the Hindu *Mahabharata*. In it, King Yudisthira is granted entry into heaven, but not his faithful dog. With tears in his eyes, the king begs, "This hound has eaten with me, starved with me, suffered with me, loved me! Must I desert him now?" And has it not been true for all societies, all peoples, that their dogs have eaten with them, starved with them, suffered with them, and loved them?

The dog is the only nonhuman species that unreservedly accepts us as we are. To a dog, we can do no wrong. All our friends may desert us—but never our dog. Its love is unconditional. Even when we mistreat it, it just looks at us through wounded eyes, unable to understand how its beloved master could reward its love and devotion with cruelty.

The ways of a dog

No American has ever lived who more totally espoused the dog, both as a species and a friend, than did Albert Payson Terhune (1872–1942), author of *Lad* and so many other books and stories about dogs and their relationships with us. One of the most informative and insightful dog-related articles I've ever come across is his "The Ways of a Dog" (*Ladies' Home Journal*, September 1919). Here are some of his conclusions:

"At four hundred yards, no dog can tell, by sight, his master from a stranger. That is why a dog first makes use of his miraculous sense of smell, next of his keen powers of hearing, and never of his eyesight until he has no further need of these two stronger senses. . . . When nature gives any creature two such potent senses as are the scent and hearing of a dog, she always restores the average by dulling some other sense. . . ."

Should a dog walk into a room— "even if it has been aired of all odors discernible to man,—he will know at once whether or not any of its occupants during the past few hours are acquaintances of his, where each stood or sat, and the route taken by them in entering or departing.

"In a wood or a field or along a country road there are a million smells no human can detect, but which have distinct meaning for a dog. . . . But this superhuman sense of smell may be as painful as it is advantageous. To blow a whiff of tobacco smoke into the face of a fellow man causes a momentary annoyance. To blow it into the face of a dog causes acute pain. The nostrils are tortured."

As to why dogs howl when hearing certain notes, Terhune debunks the common perception that the dog is "singing along" with it. "He is not. He is in anguish. Canine hearing is so many times more acute than is that of man that a high-pitched note has the same effect on the tympanum as would the point of a cambric needle. . . . He is not singing. He is screaming in agony."

So how much does a dog understand of what we say? "This same uncanny sense of hearing tells him of the faintest change in his master's mood. A shade of tone, which would escape a human, is not only audible but translatable to a dog." And no, he does not understand everything said to him. "At best, he understands barely one-tenth of it. But he does understand the way they say it.

"No courtier ever hung upon his sovereign's humors with half the zest that the right kind of dog lavishes on those of his master. And it is by this sense of hearing that he catches the nature of these varying moods. True, he scans and reads the face too. But the bulk of his mind reading is done by ear."

A dog's sense of hearing is so acute he can hear and sense our coming over a mile away. During the horse and buggy days, dogs quickly learned to differentiate between the sounds made by the different horses that pulled the carriages or wagons. "Then came the era of automobiles. Across the same bridge whizzed innumerable cars every day. In an incredibly short time my two dogs had learned to recognize the hum of our car's motor, and to differentiate it from any or all others."

Terhune wondered whether or not dogs have auricular powers we cannot even sense (in a key too high or too low for us to hear). He notes that his collie, Sunnybank Lad, was for years undisputed king of all his other dogs. "Then 'Lad' grew old, *very* old. Yet his domination did not weaken. But when he was nearly sixteen years of age he became deaf. Not stone deaf, but hard of hearing. From that moment his rulership over the other dogs ended."

As for barks, Terhune maintains, "To a student of such matters, a bark can express every shade of emotion from joy to terror. There is the challenging bark of a watchdog. There is the gayly trumpeting bark of a dog who sees his master after a long absence or who is about to be taken for a walk. There is the harrowing bark of the pup that meets a tortoise in mid-path for the first time, and there is the scared bark of the same pup when the turtle hisses at him." Interestingly enough, "no untamed branch of the dog family has a bark." The yap of the jackal and the yelp of the coyote bear no true resemblance. "The dog has his bark as an added attraction. It takes the place of no other animal sound. He has, in addition, all the vocal accompaniments of the wolf or the fox or any of the canine or semi-canine races.

"Scientific experiments in acoustics have proved that the bark of a dog has greater carrying power than has the voice of any other known animal. It is the last sound that an ascending balloonist hears after all other earth noises have died away."

Terhune also commented on the dog's marvelous sense of direction. "Many is the story of their somehow being able to find their way home across the miles. Some hundreds, some thousands." Terhune remembered a dog of his that he sold to a man who lived some distance away. Every time the dog was unchained, it found its way home. Finally, the buyer kept her tied up for two years. Then, in an unguarded moment, the dog got away and came "home" again.

Terhune also points out that a dog has only one set of weapons with which to defend itself: its teeth. "All other beasts have jaws and feet, five efficient sets of weapons, for the fending off of their foes. Man can kick or hit or bite. The cat can use her claws as well as her teeth to furious effect. And so on through the animal kingdom. The dog has his teeth alone to make him formidable. Muzzle him, and you turn him straightway into the most defenseless creature alive. A month-old kitten can out-battle him."

And if you muzzle your dog, you also "interfere with his free breathing, you cramp his sensitive mouth and lock his forty-two teeth, you mar his needful power of scent, you blur his already poor eyesight, and, worst of all, you prevent him from perspiring. A dog perspires through his tongue. That is why he pants; not because he is out of breath: it is his one means of perspiring."

As for a dog's memory, Terhune maintains that it is phenomenal and that it is directly tied to his sense of smell. "It is by scent rather than sight that your pup knows you and remembers you. It is by scent, too, that he remembers the few people he has reason to hate. . . . This memory trait is as potent for good as for ill. Not only a returning master after a long absence, but any former friend of the house whom the dog has once

←—————————————————————————————————→

accepted as a pal, can be certain of a fervid welcome. With a dog, once a friend means always a friend."

Implicit obedience, Terhune submits, is the keynote to all else a dog may be taught. But never call a dog in order to punish him, or he will cease to come when called. It is hardly ever necessary to use force in seeking compliance.

As for children, "dogs know instinctively, as a rule, who is fond of them and who is not; who fears them and who doesn't. Perhaps that may account for the abject devotion of most dogs for children, that and the knowledge of the babies' helplessness."

Terhune also addressed something I've always wondered about: Why do dogs like to go driving so much? "Nine dogs out of ten, after a single motor ride, are eager for another. Let them ride thus a few times, and the instinct is established. They love to motor. When, for some reason, they are left at home they are crestfallen and miserable. It is one of their chief joys to sit on the bumping seat of an automobile and be whizzed through the country at top speed. On such rides they do not tire and go to sleep. They survey the landscape with thrilled interest."

Terhune also pointed out that to a dog all humans are gods—and they remain so unless they prove unworthy of respect. Interestingly enough, Terhune declares that, in intellect, all dogs are roughly equivalent to two-year-old children, thus one's training methods ought to reflect that.

As to why dogs normally hate cats, Terhune suggests that it is because the dog realizes that the cat is not a domesticated animal. Furthermore, "still unconquered, loyal only to herself and scorning work or service, the cat chooses the warmest corner of the hearth and has proceeded to annex all the benefits of civilization without paying any of its penalties or taxes."

Terhune concludes by stating that the crowded city is no place for a dog, be he big or little. "If he is big, then city life is a torment to him and cuts down his already too brief span of life. A cross country romp of five minutes will give him more exercise and general benefit than will two hours of sedate walking on the end of a leash along a city street. . . . He is as bad for the city as is the city for him.

"A child who is never allowed to run or romp or play soon shows the results of such abstinence. A city-pent dog will show these results even sooner. For by nature he is still a wild beast. His love for man has domesticated him. But the strain of the wild is still there. That is why, for one thing, he turns around several times before lying down. Thus did his savage ancestors crush the stiff jungle grasses into a couch and scare therefrom any lurking snake or centipede.

"It is the throw back to the wild that makes him a watchdog. No other tame animal will give the alarm at the approach of a possible enemy. It is the wild strain in him that makes your watchdog bristle up his back and bark when he hears a strange step on your threshold. It is his loyalty which makes you and not himself the beneficiary of that instinct. It is you and your home he is defending at such times, not his own safety. He is in no personal danger from marauders, and he knows it. Otherwise he would attack or run away, not bark an alarm to warn his human god.

"And sometimes—oh, what fools we are!—if we are cross or nervous, we scold or kick a dog for his splendid protection of us. Honestly, would any human do his duty so gallantly with such scant understanding or encouragement from his master?"

The little black dog

Long ago, when I was but a child, my mother used to recite a poem titled "The Little Black Dog." I have no idea who is the author of these lines, but somehow, even after all these years, I have been able to find nothing else of comparable power—nothing else that comes so close to encapsulating the essence of a dog, and its willingness to give its all for its master:

> *I wonder if Christ had a little black dog*
> *All curly and wooly like mine,*
> *With two silky ears and a nose round and wet,*
> *And two eyes brown and tender that shine.*

←————————————————————————————→

I am sure if He had, that that little black dog
Knew right from the first He was God.
He needed no proof that Christ was divine
But just worshiped the ground that He trod.

I am sure that He hadn't, because I have read
How He prayed in the garden alone,
For all of His friends and disciples had fled,
Even Peter—the one called a stone.

And oh, I am sure that black little dog
With a heart so tender and warm,
Would never have left Him to struggle alone,
But creeping right under His arm,

Would have licked the dear fingers in agony clasped,
And counting all favors but loss,
When they took Him away, would have trotted behind
And followed Him right to the cross.

CODA

I look forward to hearing from you! I always welcome the stories, responses, and suggestions that are sent from our readers. I am putting together collections centered on other genres as well. You may reach me by writing to

Joe L. Wheeler, Ph.D.
c/o Pacific Press Publishing Association
P. O. Box 5353
Nampa, ID 83653

Owney, the Post Office Dog

Joseph Leininger Wheeler

S*trange, isn't it, how some stories just dig in their heels and refuse to die. Think of dogs, and what comes to mind? Eric Knight's* Lassie, *Jack London's* Buck *and* White Fang—*but those dogs never really existed, except in the pages of fiction. What about real dogs? The ones that stand out in memory are that great St. Bernard of the Alps, Barry; that faithful little Skye terrier, Bobby, who for over twelve years refused to leave his master's grave in Edinburgh's Old Greyfriars Churchyard—and Owney. Owney, who for almost one hundred and twenty years now, has remained part of the very fiber of the American story.*

He was immortalized in the pages of that greatest of all children's magazines, St. Nicholas. *The editors first ran a story on him in March of 1894—M. I. Ingersoll's "Owney, of the Mail Bags." The editors received so much reader feedback that a year later, in December of 1895, they published a follow-up story, Helen E. Greig's "Owney, the Post-Office Dog." But even that wasn't enough: In July of 1896, they ran a special by Charles Frederick Holder titled "Owney's Trip Around the World" (only twenty-four years after the first appearance of Jules Verne's* Around the World in Eighty Days). *These three accounts constitute the core of what we know about Owney. I am also indebted to Frank Morgan's "The Story of Owney the Dog Revisited" (Fort Lauderdale's* Hi Riser, *December 18, 2003). Some of our readers may have seen the Owney exhibit at the National Postal Museum in Washington, D. C.*

* * * * *

It all started in the Albany, New York, post office, one bitterly cold autumn day in 1888. A little puppy, tired, homeless, hungry, and shivering, sneaked into the building when a customer opened the door. Everyone being busy, no one noticed him. That gave him the courage to keep going and to slip through another momentarily opened door. In one corner of that room was a big pile of leather mailbags. Among these, the little dog found a place to curl up and promptly went to sleep.

Next morning, the postal clerks found him there when they went in for the mailbags. According to Ingersoll, "He could not tell them where he came from; but the wag of his little tail and the pleading look in his brown eyes said plainly, 'Please let me stay!' and they did."

That noon one of the post office clerks brought some soup for the puppy in a bottle from his own dinner, and the next day another kindhearted man treated him to a piece of steak.

Days went by, and nobody came to claim him. Neither did he wander away from his new quarters. He liked his new home, whatever his previous one had been, and meant to stay there. As one person and another came in and saw him, they would say:

"Whose dog is that?"

And then the postal clerks would reply, giving him a playful pat:

"Owney! Owney! who is your owner?"

After a time everybody called him "Owney."

Under good treatment Owney grew very fast and soon became a wise and intelligent little terrier. From the first night that he had slept on the mailbags he had seemed very fond of them. He often wondered, in his dog way, where the bags went to when they were tossed onto the wagons and carried off. One day he made up his mind he would go with them and see. So when the driver jumped on his high seat and drove off, Owney trotted on behind. He saw the bags flung into the railway car, and when a good chance came, he went in after them. Nobody saw him; nobody missed him. But Owney and the mailbags were old friends, and he was not afraid to go where they went. By and by, when the men began to sort the bags, they found Owney just as he had been found that first day in the office, asleep among them. They were men who knew who Owney was and where he came from, and they took care of him and brought him back on their return trip.

But Owney had learned the secret of the mailbags. Neither did he dislike the steady jogging of the train and the attention which he received. Soon after he took another trip. This time he was gone for several weeks, and his friends at Albany thought they had seen the last of him. But one morning, in he walked, looking a little thinner, a little more ragged, but very wise and happy. Though glad to be at home again, he had evidently enjoyed his trip very much. Where he had been, of course, was only conjecture, but the men at the post office thought it must have been a long distance away. His friends, afraid that he might go upon another journey and perhaps be lost, took up a subscription and bought him a collar. This collar was marked . . .

"Owney,"
Albany Post-Office,
Albany, N.Y.

To this collar was fastened a card asking the railroad postal clerks to fasten tags to him showing where he had been, if they should encounter him traveling about.

It was not a great while after this that Owney was gone again. His way of traveling was to jump aboard the first mail car he met, and when that car reached its destination and was emptied, he would take any other that was standing in the station ready to leave. If he ever got tired and wanted to go home nobody knew it, and since Owney could not ask directions as to the way back, the only thing for him to do was to keep on going.

He went to all kinds of places and met all kinds of dogs. Some days a generous postal clerk would give him a good dinner; the next day he would have none, but it was all the same to Owney so long as he had excitement and a change of scenery.

He went to Chicago, Cincinnati, and St. Louis, and the clerks attached checks to his collar. Then he went on through Salt Lake City to California, and from there to Mexico. In Mexico, someone hung a Mexican dollar on his neck. From there, Owney came up through the South, finally reaching Washington. His collar was hanging full of tags and checks, and poor Owney was weary of the heavy load about his neck. Postmaster General Wanamaker saw him and took pity on him. He took him out one day and had a harness made for him; then he took the badges from his collar and fastened them to his harness, as you see in the picture. . . .

Owney did not tarry long in Washington, but was soon off again with his new harness. The farther he went, the more checks he had to carry, and the heavier grew his load. At last the attachments alone weighed over two pounds, and poor Owney grew tired of carrying the dangling things about with him.

A Boston postal clerk saw him and took pity on him as Mr. Wanamaker had done; he carried him home to his house, and wrote a letter to the postmaster at Albany, telling him of the dog's difficulties. Word came back to take off the harness just as it was and forward it to Albany. This was done, and the harness with its attachments could be seen for years in the post office building there, preserved in a glass case with Owney's picture.

Once in his travels Owney reached Montreal, and, happening to follow the mailbags to the post office, he was taken possession of and locked up. A letter was sent to Albany telling the officials there of his whereabouts. A reply came to let him go and he would take care of himself. This the Canadian postmaster refused to do till the cost of feeding and keeping Owney was paid. In all, the bill amounted to two dollars and fifty cents. A collection was called for among his old friends, the money forwarded, and Owney released.

As the years passed, it seemed that every postal worker in America either had met Owney or had heard about him. Ingersoll described him as "a cross between an Irish and a Scotch terrier. His fur is short and curly. He has beautiful, intelligent brown eyes, but somewhere in his wanderings has lost the sight of the right one, probably from a hot cinder."

Though Ingersoll had often heard about Owney's exploits, it was not until the summer of 1893 that he actually became acquainted with him (on a camping trip): "One of our party was a postal clerk, and on the day he started for our camp Owney appeared in the postal car. My friend managed to lure the dog to our camping ground. Owney seemed pleased at first with the broad fields and enjoyed now and then a dip in the sea. But two days and two nights were enough for him. On the morning of the second day he disappeared. At half-past six in the morning Owney was still in our camp, but at half-past eight he was reported in the Old Colony Station in Boston. He must have caught the first boat for the city, and made straight for the railway station."

Ingersoll concluded his account with these words: "Where he is now, I don't know. And if I knew *today*, he might be half way to California a few days later. His home is with the mailbags, and nothing would induce him to ride in a passenger car."

By 1895, Helen Greig noted that Owney "has traveled from Alaska to Texas, from Nova Scotia to Florida, from Pennsylvania to Missouri—making side journeys and 'stop overs' as pleased him, either for rest or feeding. . . . No matter how far away he may travel, he is known as 'Owney, the Albany Post-Office Dog.'

" 'How do you know when Owney has gone on a trip?' I

asked the man who especially looks after Owney's interests.

" 'Why, when the cat comes in the office, we know that Owney is away,' he replied. 'And the dog is away from home so much, that the cat is seldom obliged to move out.'

" 'Tell me how he begins a journey. Does he know which is the postal car?'

" 'Know? Of course he does. He knows a postal car as well as any postal clerk. When the mail is sent to the station, Owney jumps on the wagon and stays there until the last bag is thrown into the car. If he feels like taking a journey, he then jumps aboard the car, barks goodbye, and away he goes. Once on the train, he is the guest of the clerks at the offices along the road.'

"He wears a fine silver collar, marked 'Owney, Albany P.O., Albany, N.Y.,' and with him is often forwarded a book in which is kept a record of places he visits; and a very interesting story the book tells.

"The first entry is 'New Westminster, British Columbia.' Then comes 'Seattle, Washington Territory.' Next, Owney was the guest of the post office at Portland, Oregon, after which he was to be found at Hardacre, Minnesota, under which name occur these lines:

> On'y one Owney, And this is he;
> The dog is aloney, So let him be.

"While he was at Bozeman, Montana, and, I fancy, a little homesick, this letter was written for him to his good friends at Albany:

> Dear Folks: I arrived here last night safe and sound from Spokane.
> I go to Helena, Montana tomorrow. I have twenty medals on my collar,
> am fat, and feel well. I start east on the 4th. I will be glad to see you all.
> Your friend, Owney.

Detroit, Michigan, contributed this short bit of doggerel:

> Owney is a tramp, as you can plainly see.
> Only treat him kindly, and take him 'long wid ye.

Baltimore joined in with this:

Once there was a dog that took it in his head
Never to stay at home, ever to roam instead.
You have him now: send him on ahead.

"At Seattle, Owney was so well treated that he stayed a long time—for him. In fact, he jumped from the postal car and returned there for another good time. A blue ribbon was attached to his collar by an admiring friend.

"A letter from the Railway Clerks' Association at Atlanta, Georgia, declares that,

Owney received an ovation here. After consenting to sit for his photograph and answering several questions, he was decorated with a medal bearing the inscription, 'Compliments of the R. R. Club,' and was carried by members to the postal car.

"Among Owney's highest trophies is a duplicate of the seal of the Postmaster General. A tag made of California tin was given to him in San Francisco.

"Postal-clerks everywhere are loud in their praises of the dog. One of them writes:

Owney is excellent company. When we arrive at stations where the train stops 'twenty minutes for refreshments,' the dog walks into the station and barks for bones. When the bell rings 'All aboard!' he is the first one on the train.

He can tell the difference between a whistle for a crossing, and that for a station; while he ignores the first, he is up and ready when the station whistle blows. He takes his place on the platform, waits until the mail is thrown off, and then goes back to bed on the mailbags.

"There was some talk of sending Owney to the World's Fair at Chicago, with all his medals, and I am sure that, on his merits, he would have taken first prize.

"At a San Francisco kennel exhibition, Owney received a very handsome silver medal as the 'Greatest Dog-Traveler in the World.'

"But the little dog is more than a mere curiosity. He is a faithful friend and companion. It is said that several times a sleepy and worn out postal clerk, who has fallen asleep, forgetful of the stations, has been wakened by Owney's barking and has thus been reminded to throw off the mailbag.

"Owney has never been 'held up' by train-robbers, but he has been in more than one wreck.

"You have heard of his wanderings—now you shall hear of his homecoming.

"When he reaches the Albany Post Office, he walks in with wagging tail, beaming with joy to be at home again. Going up to the good friend who looks after him, Owney rubs against him and licks his hands. Thus he bids all the clerks good-morning, wags his tail for a 'how-d' ye-do?' and, returning to the spot he left months ago, Owney lies down and sleeps for hours. But after this first greeting there is no familiarity.

"While in Albany, Owney goes to a certain restaurant near the post office, and then carefully selects, from the food offered, just the bones he prefers. He arrives there every day at the same hour. If the restaurant fails to supply the food that Owney is seeking, he goes to a hotel across the street, where he is sure to find a meal."

From Mr. George H. Leck, of Lawrence, Massachusetts, the photographer who took Owney's picture, comes a letter to the editor of *St. Nicholas* telling how the famous dog behaved when he sat for his portrait. At first Owney ran about the studio and seemed anxious to find a way out, but when the dog saw that a mail pouch had been placed for him to sit upon, he at once lost his restlessness and made an excellent sitter. "I had no trouble in taking all the views I wanted, as long as he was on the pouch," says the photographer.

Mr. Leck repeats a story that tells how the letter carriers of Lawrence, Massachusetts, kept Owney as an attraction for their picnic, which was to be held two weeks after Owney's arrival. The dog was very interesting to the visitors, but though his hosts treated him well, he became ugly before the end of his stay because he was kept from taking the trains.

"Owney does not like to be interfered with, and 'makes a fuss' unless he is allowed to take the first train that leaves a station. Of course the dog doesn't care where he goes, but the post office clerks like to send him where their friends will see him when he happens to get off the through lines."

Mr. Leck relates also that before the Boston Union Station was built Owney would cross the city at midnight, or any other hour, and would take little trips for himself, returning just before train time.

When Owney's picture was taken his tags were few—he had been unloaded. The dog's collar is full, and his original harness is full. Owney values his collar and knows that it introduces him to strangers in the postal service. It is easily slipped off, and he allows it to be taken off and examined; but after he has given his friends a reasonable time to study the tags, checks, and other attachments, the dog shows very plainly that he would like to have the collar put on again.

Once while the clerks were looking over the recent tags a mail train arrived, and they put down the collar to go to work on the mail. But the dog was not willing to leave his collar, and, putting his nose through it, he slipped it on for himself. After the clerks had learned of this accomplishment they often used to make Owney exhibit his cleverness by repeating the performance before their friends.

Owney's short but eventful life was now drawing to a close. But it would not be before he'd seen more of the world. Charles Frederick Holder chronicled what happened next: "You remember that Owney has traveled over almost every postal route in North America, and that tags and medals, collected from his friends along the way and amounting to a bushel or more, are kept in the Post Office Department at Washington.

"In 1895 Owney visited Postmaster A. B. Case, of Tacoma, Washington, having just returned from a trip to Alaska, and one day it happened that Owney rode down to the wharf of the Asiatic steamer, when the great vessel was taking her cargo.

"Owney was evidently much impressed with the ship's size and beauty and so plainly expressed a desire to go aboard that it was determined to send him on a flying trip around the world, and to let him break the record if possible. So, some few days later, on August 19, 1895, his friends said farewell

to Owney, as he walked up the gangway of the good ship *Victoria* of the N.P.S.S. Co., and was welcomed by Captain Panton, whose guest he was to be. Owney had his credentials in a traveling bag, and he carried also his blanket, brush, and comb, his medal-harness for full dress, and letters of introduction to the postal authorities of the world. As the steamer backed out from the dock, hundreds of people waved their hands and wished Owney a safe and prosperous voyage. So the trip began.

"Owney was soon the pet of the crew. After an uneventful voyage, he arrived at Yokohama on October 3. Here his baggage was examined, with no little curiosity, by the officials, as no dignitary had ever before entered Japan who owned so many decorations that he was obliged to carry them about with him in a bag! It was concluded that Owney must be either a dog of very high rank or the property of a distinguished person, and an account of him was promptly forwarded for the information of his Imperial Majesty, the Mikado.

"A few days later an official waited upon Owney and presented him with a passport bearing the seal of the Mikado. It was addressed to the American 'dog traveler,' and in very flowery language extended to him the freedom of the interior of the country. There were some stipulations which, in all probability, Owney would have agreed to had he made the trip. Some were as follows: 'The bearer is expressly cautioned to observe in every particular the directions of the Japanese government printed in Japanese characters on the back of the passport, an English translation of which is given herewith; and he is expected and required to conduct himself in an orderly and conciliatory manner toward the Japanese authorities and people.' The passport also forbade Owney to 'attend a fire on horseback,' warned him not to write 'on temples, shrines, or walls,' and politely requested him not to 'drive too fast on narrow roads.'

"Unfortunately, Owney had no time for side trips, and, after meeting many officials, he sailed from Yokohama, arriving at Kobi on October 9, where he received medals and a new passport from the emperor. He was at Maji, October 19, Shanghai, October 26, and Foochow, October 31, where also he received more medals and was the subject of an ovation. His fame had preceded him, and at the latter port he received an invitation to visit the U.S.S. *Detroit*, which was lying in the harbor. One day the marine at the gangway of this fine man-of-war was astonished to see a be-medaled shaggy dog come up the ladder, wagging his tail and showing all the delight that a patriotic American should at the sight of the Stars and Stripes in a foreign land. The marine almost laughed as Owney stepped aboard and ran up to the officer of the deck as though he had known him all his life.

←——————————————————————————————————→

"Owney dined in the mess-room, ate plum-duff before the mast, and—I could not begin to tell you of all the good things he enjoyed. When he reached Tacoma again he weighed several pounds more than when he started, and I am confident that his trip with the boys in blue on the cruiser *Detroit* had something to do with it. When he bade his countrymen farewell, he was decorated with the ship's ribbon, and he received a letter of introduction to other officers of the Asiatic squadron from Lieutenant-Commander E. Floyd of the *Detroit.*

"From Foochow, the dog sailed to Hong Kong, where he was unfortunately delayed and prevented from making a speed record around the world. He visited the consulate, made a round of visits to the rich tea and silk merchants, and received many curious pieces of Chinese money, which were strung to his collar. From the emperor of China, Owney received a passport bearing the royal crest and dragon, permitting him to travel in the country. But Owney did not go beyond the city, and so much red tape was employed on his departure by the Peninsular and Oriental steamer that Captain Panton of the *Victoria* finally decided to take the dog traveler back to Kobi, Japan, from which port he finally sailed to New York as the guest of Captain Grant, of the steamer *Port Phillip.*

"Owney soon knew all on board, and, as on the *Victoria,* was a member of both starboard and port watches, and dined in the cabin and before the mast with equal satisfaction.

"At Singapore, Owney went ashore with an officer, to the wonderment of the natives, who, noting his decorations, concluded that he was a personage of high rank. Some of the native dogs, it is said, looked upon him with distrust, and more than once they rushed out from narrow alleys and pounced upon the Yankee dog; but it is not on record that Owney was ever defeated. On November 30, Owney sailed from Port Said, where he put to flight more native dogs. On the trip through the Suez Canal he attracted no little attention from the various vessels and from postal authorities. Many of the clerks gave Owney mementos.

"Finally, Algiers was reached, and the quaint shipping-port visited, where Turks, Nubians, and others looked upon Owney with amazement. They handled his decorations, and some, though perhaps they did not understand just why, fastened to his collar medals which were thus sent to the American people. On December 13 Owney reached St. Michaels, the beautiful port of the Azores, spending a few hours there.

"The trip from the Azores across the Atlantic was a rough one; but there was no evidence to show that Owney did not thrive in all kinds of weather. Finally the lookout of the *Port Phillip* sighted land, and a few hours later Owney's baggage was being examined by the custom house officers, who had never before seen so strange an assortment of trophies. But, having looked at his credentials, they decided that the collection of medals and tags, though representing a large amount of metal, was personal baggage, and so passed it.

"Like all distinguished persons, Owney was met by the reporters and 'interviewed.' From the bag of decorations and letters his story was probably obtained, and the news of his arrival telegraphed to Tacoma papers as follows:

> *Owney, the postal clerks' dog, has arrived at quarantine from China, having completed the circuit of the globe. The steamer will dock today, and Captain Grant will take the dog to the post office and start him on his journey westward at once.*

"As may be expected, this announcement created no little interest among the young people at Tacoma, and Owney was the hero of the hour.

"Owney arrived in New York on December 23, at noon. He was taken immediately to the post office, and after a short reception by his many friends, started again by the New York Central for Tacoma, which he reached five days later, having completed the circuit of the globe in 132 days—a rapid rate of traveling for a dog who attracted so much attention. Owney was visited by hundreds, young and old, and so universal was the demand to see him that Postmaster Case placed him on exhibition in a public hall, and people for miles around made his acquaintance.

"At the end of his trip, Owney had over two hundred tags, medals, and certificates to add to his collection. He is today, in all probability, the best-known and the most universally popular dog in the world."

That trip around the world apparently satisfied Owney's desire to travel abroad: From that time on, he appeared content to stick to the American continent.

There is a controversy as to whether or not any train Owney was traveling on ever met with an accident: Some say yes; some say no. But since postal train employees treated him as a good luck charm and even bribed him to ride on their routes, it seems evident that, generally speaking, it was good luck to have Owney aboard.

Periodically, the Albany mail clerks would remove some of his tags for safekeeping. No one knows just how many places Owney visited or how many miles he traveled. However, he collected over a thousand tags, badges, and medals from all over the world. If one counts only the fully documented trips, he still would have logged a minimum of 142,000 miles.

Frank Morgan declares that postal workers sadly realized, by late 1896 and early 1897, that Owney's age was finally catching up with him. His diet was limited to soft foods and milk. To protect Owney from harm, mail clerks sent him back to his friends in Albany, where Owney died quietly on June 11, 1897. The Albany postal workers paid a taxidermist to preserve Owney's body.

And today, in exhibits, Owney is *still traveling!*

* * * * *

The Tail of the Lobo

Penny Porter

We are conditioned to fear the very word: wolf! Images of savage, snarling, snapping, ravenous, predators closing in for the kill swiftly come to mind whenever we think of the species. Consequently, to imagine that a wolf could possibly become a friend—Dances With Wolves notwithstanding—seems preposterous. And so it was that when the mother saw her three-year-old daughter leaning over to pet a great wolf, her heart froze with fear.

* * * * *

I had just finished washing the lunch dishes when the screen door slammed and Becky, my three-year-old, rushed in. "Mommy!" she cried. "Come see my new doggy! I gave him water two times already. He's so thirsty!"

I sighed. *Another of Becky's imaginary dogs.* After our old dog died, our remote home—Singing Valley Ranch in Sonoita, Arizona—had become a lonely place for Becky. We planned to buy a puppy, but in the meantime "pretend" puppies popped up everywhere.

"Please come, Mommy," Becky said, her brown eyes enormous. "He's crying, and he can't walk."

Now, that *was* a twist. All her previous make-believe dogs could do marvelous tricks. Why suddenly a dog that couldn't walk?

"All right, honey," I said. But Becky had disappeared into the mesquite by the time I followed.

"Over here by the oak stump. Hurry, Mommy!" she called. I parted the thorny branches and raised my hand to shade my eyes from the desert sun. A numbing chill gripped me.

There she was, sitting on her heels, and cradled in her lap was the unmistakable head of a wolf. Beyond the head rose massive black shoulders. The rest of the body lay completely hidden inside the hollow stump of a fallen oak.

"Becky!" my mouth felt dry. "Don't move." I stepped closer. Pale-yellow eyes narrowed. Black lips tightened, exposing double sets of two-inch fangs. Suddenly the wolf trembled; a piteous whine rose from his throat.

"It's awright, boy," crooned Becky. "Don't be afraid. That's my mommy, and she loves you, too."

Then the unbelievable happened. As her tiny hands stroked the great shaggy head, I heard the gentle *thump, thump, thumping* of the wolf's tail from deep inside the stump. What was wrong with the animal? Why couldn't he get up? Of course! Rabies! Hadn't Becky said, "He's so thirsty"? My memory flashed back to the five skunks who last week had torn the burlap from around a leaking pipe in a frenzied effort to reach water during the final agonies of rabies.

I had to get Becky away. "Honey." My throat tightened. "Put his head down and come to Mommy. We'll go find help."

Becky got up, kissed the wolf on the nose and walked slowly to my outstretched arms. Sad yellow eyes followed her. Then the wolf's head sank to the ground.

With Becky safe in my arms, I ran to my car parked by the house and sped to the barns where Jake, one of the cowhands, was saddling up. "Jake. Come quickly. Becky found a wolf in the oak stump near the wash. I think it has rabies."

Back at the house I put my tearful child down for her nap. "But I want to give my doggy his water," she cried.

I kissed her and gave her some stuffed animals to play with. "Let Mommy and Jake take care of him for now," I said.

Moments later I reached the oak stump. "It's a Mexican lobo, all right," Jake said, "and a big one!" The wolf whined, and then we both caught the smell of gangrene.

"Whew! It's not rabies," Jake said. "But he's sure hurt bad. Shall I put him out of his misery?"

The word "yes" was on my lips, but never spoken. Becky emerged from the bushes. "Is Jake going to make him well, Mommy?" She hauled the beast's head into her lap once more. She buried her face in the coarse, dark fur. This time I wasn't the only one who heard the thumping echo of the lobo's tail.

That afternoon my husband, Bill, and our veterinarian came to see the wolf. Observing the trust the animal had in our child, Doc said to me, "Suppose you let Becky and me tend to this fella together." Minutes later, as child and vet reassured the stricken beast, the hypodermic found its mark. The yellow eyes closed.

"He's asleep now," said the vet. "Give me a hand here, Bill." They pulled the massive body out of the stump. The animal must have been five and a half feet long, and well over one hundred pounds. The hip and leg had been mutilated by bullets. Doc peeled away the rotten flesh. He dug out bone splinters, cleaned the wound, and gave the wolf a dose of penicillin. Next day he returned and inserted a metal rod, replacing the missing bone.

"Well, it looks like you've got yourselves a Mexican lobo," Doc said. "They don't tame real easy. I'm amazed at the way this fella took to your little gal."

Becky named the wolf Ralph and carried food and water to the stump every day. Ralph's recovery was not easy. For three months he dragged his injured hindquarters by clawing the earth with his front paws. From the way he lowered his eyelids when we massaged the atrophied limbs, we knew he endured excruciating pain, but not once did he ever try to bite the hands of those who cared for him.

Four months later, to the day, Ralph finally stood unaided. His huge frame shook as long-unused muscles were activated. Bill and I patted and praised him. But it was Becky to whom he turned for a gentle word, a kiss, or a smile. He responded to these gestures of love by swinging his great bushy tail like a pendulum.

As his strength grew, Ralph followed Becky all over the ranch. Together they roamed the desert pastures, the golden-haired child often stooping low, sharing with the great lame wolf whispered secrets of nature's wonders. When evening came, he would return like a silent shadow to his hollow stump.

As he wandered the ranch, Ralph never chased the cattle. However, his excessive drooling when I let my chickens run loose prompted Bill to build a fenced-in poultry yard.

And what a watchdog Ralph was! Feral dogs and coyotes became only memories at Singing Valley Ranch. Ralph was king.

Becky's first day of school was sad for Ralph. When the bus left, he refused to return to the yard. Instead, he lay by the side of the road and waited. When Becky returned, he limped and tottered in wild, joyous circles around her. This welcoming ritual remained unchanged throughout her school years.

Although Ralph seemed happy on the ranch, he disappeared into the Santa Catalina Mountains for several weeks during the spring mating season, leaving us to worry about his safety. This was calving season, and fellow ranchers watched for the coyote, the cougar, and, of course, the lone wolf. But Ralph was lucky.

Year after year we wondered about his mate and the pups he undoubtedly sired. We learned that the wolf returns to his mate to help feed the young. We wondered how much of Ralph's own food he dragged off to his hidden family. Each June, Becky gave him extra food because he grew so thin.

During Ralph's twelve years on our ranch, the habits of his life became rituals, and his love for our child never wavered. At last the spring came when he returned home with another bullet wound. The day after Ralph's injury, some ranchers whose land bordered ours told us they'd killed a big she-wolf. The mate had been shot at also, but he kept running.

Becky was fifteen years old now. She sat with Ralph's head resting on her lap. He, too, must have been about fifteen and was gray with age. As Bill removed the bullet, my memory spun back through the years. Once again I saw a chubby three-year-old stroking the head of a huge black wolf.

The wound wasn't serious, but Ralph didn't get well. Precious pounds fell away, and his trips to the yard in search of Becky's loving companionship ceased. All day long he rested quietly. But when night fell, old and stiff as he was, he disappeared into the hills. And each morning his food was gone.

The day came when we found him dead in front of the oak stump. The yellow eyes were closed. A lump in my throat choked me as I watched Becky stroke his shaggy neck, tears streaming down her face. "I'll miss him so," she cried.

As I covered Ralph with a blanket, we were startled by a strange rustling sound from inside the stump. Becky looked inside. Two tiny yellow eyes peered back, and puppy fangs glinted in the semi-darkness. Ralph's pup! The motherless pup he had tried to care for alone.

Had a dying instinct told Ralph his offspring would be safe here, as he had been, with those who loved him? Hot tears spilled on baby fur as Becky gathered the trembling bundle in her arms.

"It's all right . . . little . . . Ralphie," Becky murmured. "Don't be afraid. That's my mom, and she loves you, too."

Did I hear a distant echo then? A gentle *thump, thump, thumping*—the tail of the lobo?

* * * * *

"The Tail of the Lobo," by Penny Porter. Published April 1984 in *Reader's Digest*, and in Porter's anthology, *Heartstrings and Tail-Tuggers*, (Ravenhawk Books, 1999). Reprinted by permission of the author. *Reader's Digest* has published more of Penny Porter's true-life animal stories than those of any other author. Today, she lives and writes from her home in Tucson, Arizona.

The Inhumanities

Julia Tavenner M'Garvey

Everything he owned was fair game for his sisters; nothing was ever where he left it. But giving away Chum without asking him—that was the last straw!

* * * * *

"U h-huh! Been sharpening my soft pencil again, haven't you?" Kent swept down belligerently on the library table where his sisters' study materials were spread out. He pounced upon a three-inch stub and snatched it unceremoniously from between the *First Principles of Latin Grammar* and a smaller volume entitled *The Inhumanities of Parents*.

"Now, look here, sis!" he began in outraged tones. "Look here!"

Elinor's eyes came slowly to focus upon the excited boy before her. Very deliberately she lowered *Genetic Psychology* and laid it down upon the *Inhumanities*.

"Quietly now, quietly," she warned him in the exasperatingly soft voice of sisterly remonstrance. "I was just making out my character trait chart for my lecture on . . ."

" 'Parental discipline,' " Kent cut in. " 'Fitting the child or making the child fit.' " He shifted easily from an exaggeratedly oracular pose to one that was mincingly feminine, taking off on Elinor's platform manner with a small boy's impish genius. " 'Help the child to help himself.' " Dropping suddenly to a normal tone, he repeated the title of Elinor's favorite lecture with ringing scorn. " 'Help the child to help himself!' You're right there with the goods all right. 'Help yourself' is some middle name for you. But will you kindly tell me what you were doing with my pencil?"

Elinor's response came sweetly unruffled. "I was using it to draw the dividing lines in my character trait chart. They have to be broad, and . . ."

"Then, in the name of mud, what did you sharpen it for?"

"Because it was worn to the wood, Kent," Elinor explained painstakingly.

"Worn to the wood!" he snorted. "I'd just got it down to make a mark like a carpenter's pencil. Now you've . . ."

The mass of brown curls on the opposite side of the table came up with a snap from the peregrinations of Caesar. "For goodness sake, Kent! No wonder I never see a bed before eleven. Who could study . . ."

"Now you butt out of this, Brownie." Kent whirled upon Grace and brought the hated nickname out roundly. "Just you . . ." He stopped short and stood for a moment staring intently. "Well, what do you know about that! What do you know about that!"

Startled, Grace looked hastily down at the spot beneath her chin where his eyes seemed glued, rapidly surveying the smart little blue-and-white tie knotted beneath her white sailor collar, and looked up blankly to meet his stare. "Well?" she challenged.

"Well?" he shouted back. "My Indian head pin! Can you beat that?"

"Oh, is that all?" said Grace with a shrug. And then as her brother stood gaping, apparently lost for words at last, she added, "Stingy! Didn't I lend you my sterling bulldog head?"

"Sure, you *loaned* it," he retorted. "I didn't just take it, did I?"

"I was almost late," Grace defended herself. "I broke my opal yesterday; and you haven't worn your old Indian pin for months."

"I wouldn't have minded about your wearing it," Kent argued. "But I promised it to Jimmy O'Herron today. His class was having an Indian drill—visitors invited. I spent twenty minutes this morning pawing through my junk looking for it. I just squeaked through the door as the tardy bell rang."

←————————————————————————————————→

"I'm sorry," Grace apologized easily. "I didn't suppose it would make any difference." With an unmistakable air of closing an unpleasant discussion she opened the *First Principles of Latin Grammar* and began softly mouthing, *"Amo, amas, amat."*

After a moment's hesitation, Kent grunted ungraciously and stalked off with his precious stub. But it was too dark now to work, so he flung the recovered pencil disgustedly into his tool box and started for the kennel.

Except during the last three weeks, Lassie had been at his heels for two years, ever since he had brought her home, a squatty little collie pup, purchased with the earnings of a summer vacation. But now Lassie had more pressing duties, even, perhaps, more wonderful pleasures, than romping with him or sitting watching him hammer nails, drive screws, and convert boards into heaps of sawdust. For Lassie, life had now become a matter of lying stretched at full length while soft little bodies tumbled over her and tiny cold noses poked continuously into her soft hair. Though she no longer followed Kent around, her eyes were even more full of their joyous welcome and an exultant pride, which he understood as clearly as words to mean, *Now, my friend, you may sit and look at my accomplishments, and I assure you it is well worth while.*

Yes, he could always find a welcome at that kennel. He whistled cheerily, expectant. Lassie had ten children, but only Chum knew Kent's whistle as far as the pert little ears could hear it. Chum always came happily to meet him, padding along awkwardly on his big, uncertain feet. Where was the little runt? "Chum!" Kent called. "Hello there, Chum!" But no answer followed his call. No tan fur came wobbling to meet him, wagging its little promise of a tail ecstatically. Kent whistled and called again, insistently, a little anxiously. Still there was no response. At a bound he took the few remaining steps to the kennel and looked solicitously down upon the peaceful family. Chum was nowhere to be seen.

Puzzled, Kent reached down into the family tangle and suffered his hand to be caressed by nine moist, black-tipped noses. But where was his own most particular tenth, the tiny, cold tan nose that always found its way into his hand first? Surely Chum was too big for Lassie to smother. Yet he pulled her to her feet almost roughly. But no, Chum was not there. He stood looking round the kennel stupidly. "Where in the name of mud . . ."

A sudden prophetic light sent him tearing toward the house. He tripped over a basket of clothespins, scattering them in every direction, and kicked a hole through a glass jar that was sterilizing on the back porch. Stumbling over a rug in the kitchen and taking a corner of the dinner cloth half way around the dining table as he passed, he landed in the library with the force of an exploding shell.

"Where's Chum?" he gasped hoarsely. Then as the family dropped their various occupations to stare at him, he translated his question desperately into language he felt that they could comprehend: "Has anybody done anything with one of my pups?"

Mr. Gregg lowered the *Evening Star.* "Why, yes, Kent. I came out this afternoon and got one of them for Johnson. He was running up to spend a weekend with his sister and had to take something for the children. He spoke about paying for it, but I wouldn't let him, of course. I imagine you will have to give the rest of them away, but, if you can sell, I'll make this one up to you."

Make it up to him! The irony of the promise! "I don't want money," the words rasped out bitterly. "I want *him.*"

Mr. Gregg laid the *Evening Star* across his knees and adjusted his voice to the customary now-do-be-reasonable tones. "Great Scott, Kent!" he expostulated. "This isn't a dog farm. You don't think we can keep ten pups!"

"You promised I could keep one," the boy began.

"What's the matter, haven't you nine?"

Kent felt too sick to cope with the rising irritation in the parental voice. "Oh, what's the use?" he cried with a hopeless choke in his voice and stamped out the way he had come.

If Elinor could have looked into his heart, she would have analyzed his feelings and charted them forthwith as "The struggle for individuality and the means of self-expression." But, knowing child welfare only from the personal point of view, Kent merely clenched his fists and muttered through shut teeth, "He had no right, no right." He stuck his clenched fists into his pockets, hunched his shoulders, and stumped round to the shed and to his bicycle.

"Kent," he heard his mother calling. "Come to dinner."

But Kent flung himself upon his bicycle and rode recklessly away into the dark. And the blackness of the night was a pale gray compared with the blackness in the boy's mind and heart. It had been like this ever since he could remember. Nothing of his was ever safe. Anything that the girls wanted they "borrowed" without asking, and the things they did not care for they dubbed "rubbish" and used for kindling. But this was the worst yet.

Lassie was his. He had bought her with his own money, the money he had earned taking care of Allen's garden from April to September. Chum was his. Even Lassie had turned her back upon her little runt. She had seemed quite blind to the pure tan nose and the saucy ears, had merely sniffed at the undersized body, and left her despised child to fight its unequal battle alone. Always he had found the poor runt at the bottom of the squirming mass of pups, except when it was nosing about among more fortunate brothers dining sumptuously under maternal approval. He had scolded Lassie roundly for an unnatural mother. But Lassie had merely rolled over with a what-do-you-know-about-children grunt and started licking that big, black-nosed bounder all over again.

Then he had taken the matter into his own hands. "Feed your baby every three hours, not every time it cries," Elinor had rehearsed all over the house the week before her lecture to the Cow Hollow Mothers' Club. So every three hours he had fished Lassie's starving baby out from under whichever of his brothers happened to be above him, pulled Black Nose away from the dinner the glutton was always greedily gobbling, and put the little runt where, in very shame, Lassie *had to* feed him. How quickly the little chap had learned the touch of Kent's fingers! In two days' time every wriggle showed gratitude. Then one morning a misty blue-black eye had peered through a crack straight up into his face with a comical eagerness that had made him chuckle out loud. "Look like my picture, old Chum?" he had asked.

From that day the runt had been "Chum." The rest of the litter were puppies—good looking enough as their eyes grew brighter and their coats more fluffy—but after all, just pups. Chum, like Lassie, was human. *Would they give Lassie away, too, some day without even mentioning it to him? he wondered. Was it to be like this forever? Was nothing that belonged to him ever to be really his? Why couldn't they occasionally be generous with someone else's things? Why not let Johnson have Grace's new tennis racket to amuse the kids, or those precious Montessori gimcracks of Elinor's? What was the use? What . . .*

A sudden jolt, a smashing sound, and he spilled out into the middle of the road. He picked himself up a little shaken, but not much hurt. His bicycle, however, was more vitally injured. "On the bum," he classed it. After a brief examination, he started for home on foot, dragging the useless machine beside him.

He dragged it through the back way and stole as noiselessly as possible into the shed, thus missing the after-dinner family council. He lighted his smoky oil lamp and placed it carefully where its flame could not be seen from the kitchen window. Then he took an inventory of the damage. He found a punctured tire, a bent axle, several broken spokes, and a few other minor casualties.

Too emotionally drained for the usual comments on his luck, he pulled open his tool chest and started to repair the wreck. The screwdriver he needed was missing. He tried one that was too big, discarded it for one that was too small, and finally managed to detach the broken parts. Then he reached for the oil can. That, also, was missing. "Sewing-machine oil run out," he muttered grimly and looked for his jar of lubricating vaseline. But that was no easier to find than the oil can.

His mouth set in a hard line. With a dry cloth he wiped the dirt from his machine and started to reassemble it. But now neither screwdriver would work. In perspiration and wrath he tried first one and then the other. Then in desperation he flung them both on the floor and started toward the house on a silent hunt for the necessary tool.

←——————————————————————————————————→

He crept quietly up on the back porch and felt hopefully over the cover of the icebox. Yes, there it was, right on top. But by the light of the library window he found it to be only his chisel, which had recently served as an ice pick.

Guess again, was his mental comment. *Sewing-machine drawer, I suppose.*

He walked to the front of the house, shinnied up a post to the upstairs porch, let himself in through a window, and made his way quietly into the sewing room. He pulled out each machine drawer and looked over the sewing table carefully. No screwdriver. But his oil can was there; also an awl that "they" frequently borrowed when the band had to be cut and tightened. He dropped these recovered properties into his pocket beside the chisel and turned next to the bathroom.

The medicine chest was first. One jar of vaseline! He added that also to his collection, muttering half aloud, "Burned fingers. But where the double dickens is that screwdriver? Now, where is it?"

Why, of course! Hadn't he seen a freshly opened can of peas on the kitchen table when he was hunting for his pencil? No wonder there was never an edge or a point on any of his tools. What was the use of sharpening and polishing? What was the use of anything?

The hurt in his heart turned suddenly to rage. He rushed down the back stairs three at a bound and tramped scowling through the kitchen and into the pantry.

"It's eight o'clock," his mother began accusingly. "Where in the world have you been, Kent?"

The girls left their work in the library to appear at the kitchen door.

"Lots of study time you'll have tonight," Grace announced. "Another fifty-eight in spelling tomorrow. You do love to write words ten times. That's what you always tell us when you're doing it."

"Habit formation," Elinor said thoughtfully, "is supposed to be governed by the favorable or unfavorable results of our acts. Even a sea anemone reacts to favorable or unfavorable stimuli, but you seem to lack its intelligence."

Kent did not turn his head in the direction of that attack, but swung himself up, planting both feet on the second shelf, and began digging round among the cans of fruit on a level with his eyes.

"Psychologists tell us . . ." Elinor was continuing.

But Mrs. Gregg interrupted sternly. "Kent," she cried, "take your feet off that shelf. How many times have I told you not to climb up there? Come down this minute."

And Kent did come down that minute, precipitately, landing flat on his back on the floor. With Kent came a crock of bread dough set to rise. It rose out of the crock in a straight line to the ceiling. It descended in almost a straight line, but only almost, for instead of falling again into the crock it fell upon Kent. It struck him full in the face—a cold, sticky mass that closed his eyes, his nose, and his mouth. In his own vernacular it "winded him" absolutely.

"Oh, my whole week's sponge!" Mrs. Gregg wailed. "As many times as I've told you not to climb up there! What were you doing in my pantry anyhow? I don't see anything funny about it, girls"—that to the girls who were standing in the doorway, with their arms now wrapped round each other while they gave way to ecstasies of gurgling squeals. "What were you doing in my pantry, Kent? What in the world did you want in there?"

Kent scrambled to his feet. With one hand he scraped enough of the mass out of his eyes to be able to glare through it. With the other he freed his mouth.

"What'd I want in there?" he stormed, pointing an accusing finger at a small, dark object mixed up with the dough on the floor. "Just my screwdriver! My screwdriver! Do you get that? My screwdriver! 'Tain't a can opener."

A big piece of dough that had been clinging to his front hair slid off, traveled down his nose, and dropped across his mouth. He exhaled in a sputtering breath that brought a fresh spasm of chokes, gurgles, and shrieks from the doorway. He turned savagely in that direction.

"You cut that out, you two stewed prunes!" he shouted. "You cut it out, I tell you! And you keep your fingers out of my boxes and let my

←——————————————————————————→

things alone! Understand? I'm through standing for it, I am!"

With the sleeve of his coat he brushed the pasty stuff away from his eyes, bringing another wail of protest from his mother.

"The only thing you let alone is my toothbrush," he raged on. "And you'll be scouring your silver manicure sets with it next, I'll bet a house. My screwdriver's mixed up with the fruit cans, my chisel's in the icebox, my lubricating vaseline's in the medicine chest, and . . ."

Mr. Gregg appeared behind the girls. "Kent," he demanded, "what's all this racket about? I'm surprised, my son. At least be a man . . ."

At the sound of his father's voice, Kent, from long habit, had cut his tirade short and contented himself with merely glowering at the new enemy. But the last admonition was too much. "Oh, you would, now, would you?" he jeered. "Be a man! Fat chance I've got, don't I? Pretty soft, bein' a man. I wish I was!"

"That will do, my son," the parental voice was forcibly parental. "We've had about enough of this disgraceful conduct for one evening."

Kent was shaking with a blinding frenzy of rage that left him no choice but to go on. "Oh, I'm bad," he flung back madly. "I'm bad, all right. But I don't go giving away things that don't belong to me."

Now the parental voice became angrily man-to-man: "Don't be a fool, Kent. You have nine pups now and . . ."

"Sure, I've got nine pups," Kent fairly howled. "Nine pups that I don't want. Out of ten pups you managed to pick the only one that I cared a hang about. That's you."

The parental voice sounded less positive, even slightly troubled. "Why, you didn't intend to keep that little runt, did you? I picked him out because I knew you were planning to sell, and I thought he would do just as well for the children to play with."

"Little runt!" Kent groaned. "Do for the children to play with! I guess yes! Of course you didn't notice how his ears stood up. Of course you didn't see that out of the ten he was the only one without a black spot on his nose. The rest of them have just found out they're alive, while he's known my whistle for days and . . ."

His voice broke in a startling manner; his eyes stung with sudden, unexpected tears; fearful of a greater ignominy than flight, he charged abruptly for the back stairs and his room.

* * *

Coming home from school the following afternoon, Kent flung himself heavily on the couch in his den and kicked the Indian chief who did duty as a pillow squarely in the face. The day had been blue funk. Enough failure marks to kill the whole week! But what did it matter? What was the use of anything?

As he stared morosely across space toward his dresser, an unfamiliar group of objects lying there attracted his attention. He rose indifferently and strolled across for a better look. His Indian pin! But where did they find the links? It had been months since he had "torn the place up by the roots" looking for them. He picked them up idly. But they were not his links; they were new, new beyond a doubt. As he stood surprised for a moment out of his gloom, he noticed something else lying on the other side of the pin—a big, broad, unsharpened carpenter's pencil.

The ache that had been in his heart all day seemed to rise to his throat in big lump. The girls were good old sports after all. They just didn't understand. He looked dully down upon the peace offerings. Well, grouching wouldn't help. He drew a deep breath.

Might as well decide which one of the pups he was going to keep. Not Black Nose, that was a cinch. Probably the one with the cute markings from his white collar down the middle of his ears or maybe the one most like Lassie. Might as well go down and have a look at them. He swallowed the lump in his throat, picked up his cap, and started out.

Crossing the yard, he tried to whistle a few favorite notes, but the rest was dirgelike. He swung into the words hastily and noisily:

"We don't know where we're going,
But we're on our way."

←————————————————————————————————→

The last word ended in a gasp. A forlorn little figure was crawling through the door of the kennel. It stood hesitating timidly. Kent rubbed his eyes and looked, looked and rubbed his eyes again. Was he seeing things? Could anything else in the world look so much like Chum?

At a bound, the boy was peering down at Lassie, peacefully sleeping, surrounded by her family. He counted them hurriedly. Nine. He counted them slowly, carefully. Nine. He turned to the little creature at his feet, gazing up uncertainly into his eyes. Poor Chum! Evidently life had proved a complex problem for him. Kent knelt down and took the poor, confused puppy into his arms. As the boy's face broke into radiant joy, Chum's eyes glistened with reflected happiness, and the tiny tail began to wag contentedly. Yet Kent still felt dazed. One half of his brain told him he must wake up soon while the other half was busily revolving stories he had read about dogs finding their way back from impossibly distant places. But, looking down at Chum's awkward, untried legs, he told himself that the very idea was preposterous. Could Lassie have searched out her missing child and brought him home? Not Lassie. Chum's welfare was the least of her worries.

The solution came in a flash. He had been too wretched to give a second thought to the sound of his father stirring around in his room before daylight that morning. In sullen indifference he had heard the front door close. And Father had been taking the six-thirty train into the country to bribe the children into giving up their new plaything so that he could bring Chum home.

Kent dropped his smooth cheek down against Chum's soft, sleek coat. It was only a tiny, tan pup that he held in his arms, but just the same, the whole universe lay embraced in that one great, heart-satisfying hug.

* * * * *

"The Inhumanities," by Julia Tavenner M'Garvey. Published September 15, 1921, in *The Youth's Companion* and November 21, 1922, in *The Youth's Instructor*. Text printed by permission of Joe Wheeler (P. O. Box 1246, Conifer, Colorado 80433) and Review and Herald Publishing Association, Hagerstown, Maryland. Julie Tavenner M'Garvey wrote for turn-of-the-twentieth-century popular and inspirational magazines.

The Killer

Verne Athanas

The boy had no mother and no father—and longed for a dog. But neither his uncle nor his aunt would permit him to have one.

Then along came Josef and Karl from Croatia—and Vuki.

* * * * *

Sometimes we forget that God made other breeds of men—and dogs—than those we have grown up with.

Josef Kosnic was different enough, by himself. He came from the hills of Croatia, and the flavor of his homeland was on his tongue, which set him apart almost instantly. He also raised goats, another peculiar item by the standards of the day. Then there was his brother Karl—and the dog— but that came later.

I was going on thirteen when Josef Kosnic moved into the old DeGraaf place with his goats and his dog. He'd got the place through the agent in Milton, the county seat then, fifteen miles away. He was a stocky man, Josef Kosnic, weathered brown face and a big bushy mustache, and keen little brown eyes that hid behind squinted lids under bushy, overhanging eyebrows. A quiet man, without much speech, which may have come from his difficulty with this language of ours.

←——————————————————————————————————→

I guess the first time I ever paid much attention to him was when he came through town one morning. Ed Frohmann was standing on the front porch of Glover's store, and he chuckled and said to Mark Glover, "Mark, you'd better lock up. Here come the gypsies."

He was quite a card, Ed Frohmann, always ready with a clever remark. He was big and tall, with a round face and a substantial belly on him, though I don't think he was more than thirty-five then. He was a pretty big landholder and the town constable—which was more or less an honorary office, because Weaver was about as free of crime as any other village in the country those days. That is to say, somebody missed a chicken once in a while, and about once a month Ed had to go down to the tavern and get Amos Broadfoot and lock him up overnight in the back room of the town hall.

Ed used to laugh about that. He'd make Amos sweep out the town hall next morning, and then he'd turn Amos loose. Ed used to say, "If Amos ever takes the pledge, it's going to cost the town money, 'cause we'd have to get a janitor for the town hall. I figure he saves the town five dollars a month, regularly."

But, as I say, Ed was the town constable, the only public official we had, except for Judge Vernon, who was the justice of the peace. Ed carried a pistol in a special holster that was set down into his hip pocket so that all you saw was the curved butt of it sticking up in back. Just a kind of a politician's position, you might say, and Ed didn't even wear a badge. Carried it around in his shirt pocket, but he didn't have to show it twice a year. Everybody knew Ed and what he was.

So when he made this crack about the gypsies coming, he laughed, and I took my first look at Josef Kosnic.

There was something to what Ed said, in a way. Josef had fixed up an old buggy, but he hadn't had much to work with, and the four wheels leaned in four different directions. He'd bought that old bay mare that Voss Greener had been trying to pawn off on somebody for three years, and the harness was as old as the buggy, though you could see he'd oiled it and patched it up.

But it was the dog that caught my eye. I'd never seen anything like it in my thirteen years. It looked like a cross between a greyhound and a white collie, but bigger. Long slender head, ears well back, thick chest and no belly at all. It was trotting along behind the buggy, not looking around, like most dogs, but tending strictly to business.

Josef pulled up and got down and came into the store, nodding to everybody, and he bought cheese and crackers and a couple of tomatoes from Glover. The dog had flopped out directly under the rear axle of the buggy, and lay quietly, head up proudly and alertly, but without letting on that there was a thing in the world around him. Like a kid will, I walked over toward him and spoke.

He turned his head and looked at me—and that was all. Not a twitch of his ears, not a move with his tail. I wanted to reach out and feel his silky-looking ears, but somehow I didn't have the nerve.

Then Josef Kosnic came out, and I dug up words and asked, "What kind of a dog is he?"

Kosnic put his packages carefully under the seat and said in his odd-flavored tongue, "Borzoi. How you say? . . . Roos-ian volf hount."

"What's his name?"

Kosnic smiled again. "Vuki. Like you say . . . Volf."

"That's a funny name," I said, the way a kid will. "Vuki."

Kosnic said mildly, "You say *Volf*, my country sounds funny too." You know, that gentle little reproof was the first time I really realized that maybe foreigners are people, too. Sure, if I said "Wolf" to the people who knew it was "Vuki," well, maybe they'd look at me like people here looked at Kosnic.

"Vuki," I said, to sort of cover up what I was thinking, and I snapped my fingers at the dog. He ignored me.

Kosnic was watching me. "You like pat him?"

"Is it all right?"

"Sure," he said. He said something to the dog in his language, and the dog stood up and came to us. I ran my hand across his flat narrow head, and he felt just as silky as he looked, but he didn't lean into my patting, and he didn't wag his tail. His shoulders came nearly up to my waist.

"Wow," I said, "He's sure a swell dog. What kind, did you say again?"

"Borzoi," said Kosnic.

Ed Frohmann chuckled right behind me. "Looks more like a pantry setter to me," he said.

I said real quick, so Kosnic wouldn't pay any attention to Ed, "He's a swell dog."

Kosnic said, "Sure," and got into his buggy. He didn't pay any attention to Ed, and neither did the dog.

When he drove off, Vuki trotted right along behind, following the buggy. Ed sort of shrugged and walked back to the porch of the store.

It was the afternoon of the same day that Karl came. That's where Josef Kosnic had been going, I found out later, over to Milton to meet the train and get Karl.

We didn't pay too much attention to Karl that afternoon, because of what happened. But we did see that he was taller than Josef, but thinner, and he was cleanshaven. He wore a blue suit and black shoes and a gray hat, all of them new and stiff and cheap, and he never got out of the buggy seat.

But that wasn't the big part of the afternoon. Ed Frohmann came up the street with his dog. He'd taken a lot of joshing about that dog, but Ed would never admit he'd got stung.

It was an English mastiff, and Ed had bought him about a month before and paid quite a price for him. He hadn't owned him three days before everybody knew Ed had a spoiled dog. Even Ed, big as he was, couldn't handle him without a choke collar and a chain.

He was big, and he was bad. There'd been a lot of guessing and betting on his weight, so finally one day they muzzled him, and tied him, and flopped him on the scales in front of the store, and he tipped the beam to just a little over a hundred and fifty pounds. That's a lot of dog, even for a mastiff.

Well, Ed came up the street with his dog on a chain. I wondered a lot about that afterward—whether or not he'd figured on Kosnic coming back, or what. But he and the mastiff were on the porch at Glover's when Josef and Karl came through.

Ed said afterward that his dog pulled loose when he saw Vuki. I don't know. But just as the buggy came even with the porch, Ed's mastiff went charging out into the street heading straight for Vuki.

That's when Josef surprised us all. He came down over the wheel of the buggy quicker than you'd think possible, and he grabbed the buggy whip out of the socket as he came. He said something in his language to Vuki, and the wolfhound stopped stock still, not moving a muscle.

Josef met the mastiff at the rear wheel, and the whip began to pop and sing around that mastiff's ears. It was close. For a second, I thought the mastiff was going to take Josef, but the whip finally drove him back.

It took more than I'd have had. The mastiff had a head like a bull, and considering his fighting fire, those wicked jaws working and slobbering, eyes mean and red behind squinted lids, I'd have been up on the buggy seat with something heavier to swing than a buggy whip! But Joseph Kosnic held him until Ed went after him, not hurrying either.

He got hold of the chain and said, "What's the matter, afraid your dog would get hurt?"

Kosnic looked him square in the face and said, "I am not afraid for my dog. But it is foolish thing to make them fight for no reason."

He lowered the whip, and Ed pulled on the chain. The mastiff didn't want to come. He rumbled deep in his chest and strained on the collar, and Ed jerked him sharply, so that the choke collar tightened up with a snap and jerked the mastiff's head around.

He came then, but fast, and Ed pulled back with the doubled end of the chain in his other hand, raising it, ready to hit. I guess the mastiff knew that one, for he settled back and let Ed shorten up on the chain. I saw Kosnic's lips tighten, but he didn't say anything.

Ed seemed to have trouble getting his smile to working, but he said, in

⟵————————————————————⟶

his rough, joking way, "You'd better keep your pet home. If King here ever catches him, he'll eat him up."

Kosnic said again, "Is foolish to make dogs fight." Then he climbed back into the buggy and drove on. That was when I noticed that Karl—of course I didn't know who he was then—hadn't moved.

Ed Frohmann watched the buggy go down the street, and I guess maybe it hadn't set too well with him, because he said, loud enough so we all heard, "It's a good thing King didn't get at him. Did you see the way he took that chain right out of my hand when he spotted that Rooshian animal?"

Nobody said much, and Ed finally took the dog home.

I don't know whether you'd call it kid curiosity or what, but a couple of days later, I went up to the Kosnic place. It was only a couple of miles, and I took a fishing pole with me. Indian Creek ran through a corner of the place.

They were working in their garden when I got there, both of them with hoes, chopping weeds. Josef looked up and smiled.

"You go fishing?" he asked.

I said, "If it's all right to fish in your creek."

"Sure," he said, "sure." I guess he saw me looking at Karl, for he said, "This is my brother, Karl. He comes live for me."

Karl didn't say anything. He just looked at me and bobbed his head and went on chopping weeds. He wasn't brown and weathered like Josef. His face was almost gray, and besides being cleanshaven, his hair was cut short and close to his head. The dog, Vuki, was lying in a corner of the rail fence, with his head on his forepaws.

I said, "Vuki!" and slapped my hand on my thigh. He raised his head and looked at me, but he didn't move.

Josef said something that sounded like "Dobra, Vuki," and the dog got up and came to me. I rubbed his head, and I thought I saw his tail wag just a fraction of an inch.

Josef said, "You got no dog?"

"No. My aunt don't like dogs."

"You live for your aunt?" I'd figured out now that when he said *for* like that, it meant "with."

"Yes," I said, and then, "I sure wish I had a dog like Vuki."

Josef said, "Your papa, he no get you dog?"

"I got no father," I said. I'd got to where it didn't bother me so much anymore. It had been five years now, and I'd gotten over a lot of it. I said to sort of cover up, "I'll bet no kid ever had a dog like this in this town."

Josef tugged at the end of his big bushy mustache.

"Borzoi," he said, "is not—what you call—play dog. Is—what you say—friend dog. Not for pull ears, jump and run around dog. Is like you pa—you uncle. You don't make play with him, does it? No. Shake hands like gentleman, like friend. You see?"

I saw, all right. Vuki was a gentleman. He didn't romp and run and wiggle after he was petted. I learned a lot about him as I went.

I got into a habit of going up to the Kosnic place three or four times a week. Josef was never too busy to talk to me. He showed me his goats, and after a while he let me milk one.

I ate with the Kosnics lots of times too. I learned to eat the goat's milk cheese they made, white and waxy, pickled in brine, and served up in chunks as big as your fist. They cooked up black-eyed peas with onions and a little bit of garlic and little cubes of meat wrapped in a cabbage leaf, all simmered together. Or chicken, stewed with rice, with strained tomatoes and chopped onions and bay and thyme and a half-dozen other herbs that I didn't know, all cooked up so rich and tender you could almost eat the chicken bones.

I learned a lot from the Kosnic brothers, only I didn't know then that it was learning. Karl got browner, as the summer went along and the sun worked on him. He came to know me, and while he never did talk like Josef did, he always had a smile for me, and he'd hand me things at the table and urge me to eat more.

But I think it was Vuki that I liked the most. He knew, always, when I was coming, long before I got there. He would meet me at the mailbox, stand perfectly still while I rubbed his head and scratched behind his ears, and then he'd wheel and walk beside me to the house. He never came to be touched any other time, except for that first meeting at the mailbox.

Sometimes he'd go fishing with me, lying on the bank and watching interestedly while the cork bobber drifted around in slow circles in a quiet eddy. I got so I could watch his ears and tell when the bobber was dipping. But he never made a sound or got excited, even when I'd toss a flopping chub up onto the bank within a foot of him.

It seems funny to me now that Aunt Vinnie didn't bother much about my visiting. Maybe it was a relief to her. Aunt Vinnie seemed awfully old to me then, and I suppose she might have been fifty. But she and Uncle Albert never had any children, and I suppose a boy in that dim, stiff, silent house of theirs must have taken some adjustment. Or perhaps one reason she didn't protest my constant visiting was that I'd quit pestering them about dogs and such. Certainly my manners were better.

I behaved myself very carefully, so as to give them no reason to confine me to my yard or my room in punishment. They never licked me. Sometimes I wished they would, when I'd done something that kept me penned up in my room while a long, endlessly long, afternoon crept past. It's funny, but I've never seen a day since I was fifteen that was as long as those afternoons were—quiet and drowsy and timeless, with that dusty-hot smell of leaves and unpaved roads and weathered woods—a silly thing, but that smell had excitement in it, a promise of things to do. I'll never forget it—but I've never found it again.

A lot of things changed for me that summer. You see, Vuki was the closest thing to a dog of my own I'd ever had. It got to where he seemed to like me better than he did Josef or Karl, but the only way he ever showed it was by the way he'd follow me around. He'd follow me to go fishing, and when he came to town with the brothers, following the old buggy, he'd never leave the buggy unless I happened to be around, and then he'd come to me. I guess maybe I came to love that dog more than anything or anybody.

Part of it, I suppose, was because I was sort of a lonesome kid. I'd lived in Weaver with Uncle Albert and Aunt Vinnie for only about a year, and while I went fishing with Jimmie Tolliver and played with him some, I wasn't the same to him as the kids he'd lived with and grown up with all his life. Maybe that's how this thing came to happen.

* * *

Josef came to town that day, and Jimmie and I were sitting on the porch with our feet in the dust of the street, and Rex, Jimmie's dog, was lying in the shade. Josef got down and smiled at me and went into the store, and Vuki came across the street to me. Rex stiffened up, and got up and walked stiff-legged like a dog will around another strange dog, but Vuki didn't pay any attention to him.

Rex dropped down off the porch and went out a ways, sort of stiff and strutting, and I'll never know what made Jimmie do it, but he said sharply, "Sic 'em!"

Well, Rex was a whopping big dog, a mutt with more beef than brains, of no particular breed but with lots of ancestors. He growled and took a couple of fast steps toward Vuki, and Vuki stopped.

I said to Jimmie, "You stop that!" And then Jimmie, figuring, I suppose, that stopping like that made Vuki a coward, yelled again, "Sic 'em, Rex!"

I yelled too, but it was too late. Rex charged Vuki, and Vuki gave ground. Rex charged again, and it was over that quick. Vuki made two chopping strikes with that flat narrow head of his, and Rex made a strangled screaming noise and fell over kicking. He was dead before we could move.

Vuki stood stiffly over Rex's body for a long moment, stiff and tall, and then he walked back to the buggy, dropped down, and started to clean himself up with his tongue.

←——————————————————————→

I couldn't move. I couldn't think. Jimmie was standing, too, looking at Rex, stiff and scared and still not believing it. Then I suddenly thought of Josef, inside, and I turned to get him. But he was already coming. I guess he'd heard the noise and knew what was happening. He was running.

Ed Frohmann was right behind him. I remember thinking it looked kind of peculiar, because Ed had his little girl, Nancy, in his arms, and he set her down as he came out on the porch and said quickly, "Stay here, now, Honey."

She was a pretty little thing, just three years old, with blond curls and blue eyes, a regular little doll of a girl, and Ed didn't think any more of his right arm than he did of her. He'd carry her around for hours at a time, take her with him when he went to the store, play with her, bounce her on his knee. My uncle said it just went to show that it took a lot of different kind of parts to make a man.

But I wasn't thinking of that right now. I was thinking of Ed's size and his bullying ways and the fact that he'd already had a little put out with Josef.

Jimmie was crying now and saying, "He killed Rex. He killed Rex."

I was scared, but I said, "You started it. You sicced Rex on him."

Then Ed said, "Kosnic, you got to get rid of that dog."

But Joseph looked at me and asked, "Why did this happen, Billy?" His eyes were big and steady, and he wasn't smiling under his mustache.

I said, "I told you, Jimmie sicced Rex on Vuki. Vuki tried to dodge him, but Rex kept coming."

Ed said again, sounding real tough, "You got to get rid of that dog, Kosnic, or I will. He's a killer."

"No," said Josef Kosnic. "Is not the dog's fault. Is foolish people— make the dogs fight."

Ed's face got red. He reached into his hip pocket and dragged out his pistol. "I'll take care of it myself, then," he said.

Josef Kosnic took a step forward and stood right in front of Ed. "You shoot me first then," he said. Not loud, not showing off. Just plain and straight and very, very quiet.

Ed growled at him and took a step to the side and brought up the gun, and Josef stepped square in front of it. Ed made a snarling sound in his throat, and he brought the gun back like he was going to hit Josef with it. Josef stood and looked at him without moving a muscle.

Ed stood that way a long moment. Then he lowered his hand and fumbled the gun back into his hip pocket. "You get rid of that dog," he said and turned and stomped back to the store porch.

Josef looked at me, and he tried to smile, and I tried to smile back. But it didn't work. I kept looking at Vuki, the same Vuki that followed me around, let me rub his head, and it wasn't the same at all. I kept seeing his eyes, cold and mad and slitted, and his wicked narrow jaws tearing the throat out of Rex, and all of a sudden I was shivering, and a little icy worm was crawling up my spine. Josef saw it, and he said quietly, "Billy, you ride with me a little bit. We talk for this thing."

I guess that was part of learning too. I climbed up onto the high rickety seat with Josef, and he clucked the old mare ahead. We were out of town before he spoke.

"Billy," he said, "I told you first time. Vuki is Borzoi dog. Not play dog—hunting dog. Borzoi family goes back hundred, hundred, hundred year. One reason to live, just one—to hunt, to kill. Borzoi is only dog to hunt and kill the big wolf of Siberia. Is gentleman dog, but not for play fight. Vuki—Vuki is from old family. Is inside, all this. Born inside, in the bones, in the muscles, in the brain. But he is same dog as yesterday. He like you, you like him. No different. You see?"

I did see part of it. But not all. Not enough to be able to see Vuki just as he was before. But I did see part of it. Josef patted my shoulder and stopped the mare.

"You onnerstan', Billy?" He smiled at me anxiously.

"Sure," I said. "Sure." I got down and stood by the wheel. I couldn't help it. I looked at Vuki.

He looked back. And so help me, he knew. He understood! He didn't come to me, didn't budge an inch.

I said suddenly, without knowing why, "Vuki."

I snapped my fingers. He hesitated, then came, and raised his head against my hand. I rubbed his head, scratched his silky ears. Then I ran, because I was afraid I was going to cry, and it made me mad.

Uncle Albert and Aunt Vinnie talked about it at supper. Uncle Albert looked at me that night and said in his quiet gray voice, "Isn't that the dog that belongs to the Kosnic brothers? The ones you are always visiting?"

I looked at him and back at my plate. "Yes," I said.

He didn't say anything for a while, and then he said, "I think you'd better stay home for a few days, William."

That was the only way he ever told me anything, but it was an ironclad order. I didn't say anything. I'd learned how useless it was.

It was next night at supper that Uncle Albert told us.

"Ed Frohmann," he said, "has sworn out a complaint against the Kosnic brothers and their dog. The dog killed three of Ed's sheep."

I remember I dropped my fork, because it made such a noise in that quiet room. I shouted, "He's not going to shoot Vuki!"

It startled them, and they both looked at me, and then Uncle Albert said quietly, "Perhaps not. But Ed has sworn out the complaint, and the Kosnic brothers will have to appear before Judge Vernon to show cause why the dog should not be destroyed."

I gulped and felt the supper I'd eaten making a big heavy lump in my stomach. "He didn't do it," I blurted.

I couldn't read Uncle Albert's face, but he said very quietly, "Maybe not. But I hear there were witnesses, and the dog's tracks were all around."

"But he didn't," I said, and I felt the lump in my stomach pushing at me. Uncle Albert looked at me and said almost gently, "You'd better go to your room, William."

I jumped up and shoved my chair back and ran out without saying even " 'scuse me." Uncle Albert let me go.

I had to go to the hearing. Even without permission, I had to go. It wasn't formal, like a big trial or anything like that. Judge Vernon sat at a desk in the town hall, and there were chairs in front of the desk. The door was open, for it was a stifling hot day. This was the latter part of August, and even Judge Vernon, who was always crisp and cool looking in his white shirt and neat black broadcloth coat, was mopping at his high forehead with a big white handkerchief. Josef and Karl sat on two chairs facing the desk, and Vuki lay between them, with a collar and a leash on. That was the first time I'd ever seen him under restraint, and he was feeling the heat, too, for his long pink tongue lolled out past his clean white teeth, and he panted in short gusty breaths.

I slipped in through the open door and scrunched down in a chair against the back wall. I guess things had already started, because Judge Vernon said, as I came in, "Josef Kosnic, will you stand, please?"

Josef stood up. Karl was slumped in his seat, and I could see him sideways when Josef stood, and Karl was gray looking and staring at the floor.

Judge Vernon said, "Mr. Kosnic, have you anything to say to the charges the constable has stated?"

"Mr. Judge," Josef said, "I think is mistake. Vuki not sheep killer. Maybe he kill to eat, but not for fun. But he is not hungry, and he not kill sheep."

Ed said loudly, "I suppose he killed that dog the other day because he was hungry!" He sounded mad.

Josef said quietly, "He kill dog because foolish people make the dogs fight."

"He's a killer!"

"In fight, yes." Josef was standing patiently, his arms at his sides. He did not raise his voice. "Is maybe thousand years—how you say—bred to kill in fight." He looked back at Ed. "Is made to kill, the Borzoi dog, like the pistol you carry." He shrugged, and I could see the corner of his mustache curve in a wry smile. "The pistol, it makes you killer?"

Somebody snickered, and Ed's face went brick red. He roared, "Look here, you smart-alecky bohunk . . ."

Judge Vernon snapped out, "That will do, Ed."

Ed wheeled around violently and said harshly, "I don't care, Judge. These birds think they're pretty cute. Him and his killer dog and his jailbird brother!"

I heard Karl make a sound at that, and he seemed to shrivel in his seat. Ed Frohmann spun back and demanded, "It's true, isn't it?"

Judge Vernon said quickly, "You don't have to answer that, Mr. Kosnic. It has no bearing on the case."

Josef straightened his shoulders. "Is all right. Is true. Karl no wants to come, today. He spend one year in the prison, and he is afraid for police and judges. He hit a man with his fist, and the man hit his head on a wall and was hurt. He called Karl bad name, thinks Karl is not a man to care what he is called." He put a hand on Karl's shoulder. "The man had friends. Karl, no friends. Not even speak the language good. Man lie to judge, say Karl hit him with club. Karl scared, no onnerstan', and judge say one year in the jail. So Karl is scared for America law. I'm no scared." He straightened up and looked Judge Vernon in the face. "If I honest," he said, "and you honest—America law OK."

Judge Vernon almost smiled. "You're a shrewd man, Mr. Kosnic," he said.

I don't think Josef knew what he meant, but he said, "Thank you, Mr. Judge."

Judge Vernon almost smiled again, and he leaned his elbows on the desk and clasped his fingers together.

"This is a very serious charge, Mr. Kosnic," he said, "and the constable tells me he has witnesses . . ."

Somebody yelled outside just then. I was sitting by the door, and I turned and looked up the street. For a minute, I didn't see anything, and then I spotted him.

It was King, that big mastiff of Ed Frohmann's, and he was coming down the street at a sort of a swaggering trot. It was so hot that the street was dancing with heat waves, and great ropy strings of slobber and froth were coming from King's mouth. He was swinging his head back and forth, like a bull does when he is looking for a fight, and he wasn't making a sound that I could hear. A foot of broken chain dangled from his collar.

Then I saw the little girl. Ed's baby daughter, Nancy. She was toddling out into the road, with that unsteady little run of a three-year-old, and she was heading right for that dog, waving her little hands and shrieking with excitement.

That's when I yelled and spilled out of my chair and out the door. I guess I must have said Nancy's name, because I heard a roar from Ed Frohmann, and he came charging through the rest of the spectators like a runaway locomotive.

He saw what was happening instantly. He shouldered me aside and made a dive across the porch, dragging at his pistol as he went. Weaver was still village enough then to have hitching racks in front of the porch, and Ed put one hand on the bar, to vault over, and the pole broke.

He sprawled on his side, the wind jarred out of him, and when he tried to shove himself up with one hand, something snapped, and he fell back. The gun fell out of his hand, and the sweat poured off his round face.

Then Josef Kosnic was beside me, stooping to unsnap the collar from Vuki, and he was letting out a screaming yell in his own tongue and pointing, and slapping Vuki on the flank. Vuki made a white streak up the street, in great bounding leaps that must have been ten feet to the jump. The mastiff drove in and knocked little Nancy down, and a hoarse roar came out of him as his great jaws opened. He stood like that when Vuki hit him.

It was a nightmare thing I'll remember all my days. Those two great animals reared up against each other, killers both, fighters, born and bred for a thousand generations, roaring and snarling their blood lust, and the little girl in her dust-smeared pink dress, trying to sit up beneath them.

Then Vuki's narrow wicked head struck and tore, and they came down together in a threshing tangle, and the mastiff's great bull roar sounded out. Over and over and over, they went, faster than you could see, and I remember how slow the men seemed, those running toward them.

Then another roar, with a mad bubbling note in it, and they reared up again, the mastiff big as a house, Vuki's narrow jaws jammed deep into the mastiff's throat. Then the mastiff kicked once, convulsively, and they fell apart. I was running, jumping as hard as I could go, but it was over before I got there.

Vuki went down too. He turned half away from the mastiff on crouched legs, and then he fell. I dropped on my knees beside him, and instantly his flat wicked head swung toward me, and then I spoke. His head sagged, and his ears came forward. He dragged himself to me, a crippling lurching drag, and he put his head on my thigh, and his pink tongue, bloody now, came out and left a smear on my hand. Then he died.

Ed Frohmann had Nancy cradled up in his good arm, soothing and rubbing his sweaty cheek against hers, paying no attention to his dangling useless arm. Josef and Karl were coming up the street, slowly, as if they didn't want to come, and Josef looked ten years older. But it all didn't mean a thing to me, not a thing.

I looked down at my hand and the red smear that Vuki's tongue had left on it; I looked at his head, lying dead on my thigh. He'd licked my hand. The only caress he'd ever given anybody in his life. I rubbed a silky ear between my dusty fingers.

I didn't cry. That's part of growing up, I guess, but that was the day I learned not to cry.

* * * * *

"The Killer," by Verne Athanas. If anyone can provide knowledge of the earliest publication of this old story, please send information to Joe Wheeler (P. O. Box 1246, Conifer, Colorado 80433). Verne Athanas wrote for turn-of-the-twentieth-century popular and inspirational magazines.

Wolf

Albert Payson Terhune

Even though the dog did not win medals like Lad and Bruce, the Boy felt he deserved to. To compensate, he loved Wolf all the more.

Then came a pitch-dark night.

* * * * *

There were three dogs on The Place—collies all. There was a long shelf in the master's study whereon shimmered and glinted a rank of silver cups of varying sizes and shapes. Two of The Place's dogs had won them all.

Above the shelf hung two huge picture frames. In the center of each was the small photograph of a collie. Beneath each likeness was a certified pedigree, abristle with the red-letter names of champions. Surrounding the pictures and pedigrees, the whole remaining space in both frames was filled with blue ribbons—the very meanest bit of silk in either was a semioccasional purple or white "Reserve,"—while strung along the tops of the frames from side to side ran a line of medals.

Cups, medals, and ribbons alike had been won by The Place's two great collies, Lad and Bruce. (Those were their "kennel names." Their official titles on the AKC registry list were high-sounding and needlessly long.)

←—————————————————————————————————→

Lad was a mahogany-and-white giant of a dog, with a soul that was as big as his body and as human as his deep brown eyes. He was such a dog as one meets with once in a lifetime—and seeks for, vainly, before and after.

But now he was old, very, very old. His reign on The Place was drawing toward a benignant close. His muzzle was snow white, and his once graceful lines were beginning to blur with the oncoming heaviness of age. No longer could he hope to hold his own in form and carriage with younger collies at the dog shows where once he had carried all before him.

Bruce was six years younger, tawny of coat, kingly of bearing, a dog without a fault of body or of disposition, stately as the boar-hounds that the painters of old used to love to depict in their portraits of monarchs.

The Place's third dog was Wolf. But neither cup nor ribbon did Wolf have to show as an excuse for his presence on earth. Nor would he have won recognition in the smallest and least exclusive collie show.

For Wolf was a collie only by courtesy. His breeding was as pure as was any champion's, but he was one of those luckless types to be found in nearly every litter—a throwback to some forgotten ancestor whose points were all defective. Not even the glorious pedigree of Lad, his father, could make Wolf look like anything more than he was—a dog without a single physical trait that followed the best collie standards.

In spite of all this he was beautiful. His gold-and-white coat was almost as bright and luxuriant as any prizewinner's. He had, in a general way, the collie head and brush. But an expert, at the most casual glance, would have noted a shortness of nose and a breadth of jaw and a shape of ear and leg and shoulder that told dead against him.

The collie is supposed to be descended direct from the wolf. And Wolf looked far more like his original ancestors than like a thoroughbred collie. From puppyhood he had been the living image, except in color, of a timber wolf. And it was from this queer throwback trait that he had won his name.

Lad was the mistress's dog. Bruce was the master's. Wolf belonged to the Boy, having been born on the latter's tenth birthday.

For the first six months of his life Wolf lived at The Place on sufferance. Nobody except the Boy took any special interest in him. He was kept only because all his better-formed brothers and sisters had died in early puppyhood and because the Boy, from the outset, had loved him.

At six months it was discovered that he was a natural watchdog. Also that he never barked except to give an alarm. A collie is, perhaps, the most excitable of all large dogs. The veriest trifle will set him off into a thunderous paroxysm of barking. But Wolf, the Boy noted, never barked without strong cause.

He had the rare genius for guarding that so few of his breed possess. For not one dog in ten merits the title of watchdog. The duties that should go with that office are far more than the mere clamorous announcement of a stranger's approach or even the attacking of such a stranger.

The born watchdog patrols his beat once in so often during the night. At all times he must sleep with one ear and one eye alert. By day or by night he must discriminate between the visitor whose presence is permitted and the trespasser whose presence is not. He must know what class of undesirable to scare off with a growl and what class needs stronger measures. He must also know to the inch the boundaries of his own master's land.

None of these things can be taught; all of them must be instinctive. Wolf had been born with them. Most dogs are not.

His value as a watchdog gave Wolf a settled position of his own on The Place. Lad was growing old and a little deaf. He slept, at night, under the piano in the music room. Bruce was worth too much money to be left at large in the nighttime for any clever dog thief to steal. So he slept in the study. Thus Wolf alone was left on guard. The piazza was his sentry box. From this shelter he was wont to set forth three or four times a night, in all sorts of weather, to make his rounds.

The Place covered seventeen acres. It ran from the high road, a furlong above the house, down to the lake that bordered it on two sides. On the third side was the forest. Boating parties, late at night, had a pleasant way of trying to raid the lakeside apple orchard. Now and then, tramps strayed down the drive from the main road. Prowlers, crossing the woods, sometimes sought to use The Place's sloping lawn as a short cut to the village below.

For each and all of these intruders Wolf had an ever-ready welcome. A whirl of madly pattering feet through the dark, a snarling growl far down in the throat, a furry shape catapulting into the air, and the trespasser had his choice between a scurrying retreat or a double set of white fangs in the easiest-reached part of his anatomy.

The Boy was inordinately proud of his pet's watchdog prowess. He was prouder yet of Wolf's almost uncanny sharpness of intelligence, his quickness to learn, his knowledge of word meanings, his zest for romping, his perfect obedience, the tricks he had taught himself without human tutelage. But none of these talents overcame the sad fact that Wolf was not a show dog and that he looked positively underbred and shabby alongside his sire or Bruce. This rankled at the Boy's heart even while loyalty to his adored pet would not let him confess to himself or to anyone else that Wolf was not the most flawlessly perfect dog on earth.

When this story begins, Wolf was four years old. Undersized (for a collie), slim, graceful, fierce, affectionate, he was still the Boy's darling and the official guardian of The Place. But all his four years had brought him nothing more than this—the four years that Lad and Bruce had spent in winning prize after prize at one local dog show after another within a radius of thirty miles.

The Boy was duly enthusiastic over the winning of each trophy. But always, for days thereafter, he was more than usually attentive to Wolf, to make up for his pet's dearth of prizes.

Once or twice the Boy had hinted, in a veiled, tentative way, that Wolf might perhaps win something, too, if he were allowed to go to a show. The master, never suspecting what lay behind the cautious words, would always laugh in good natured derision. Or else he would point in silence to Wolf's head and then to Lad's.

The Boy knew enough about collies to carry the subject no further. For even his eyes of devotion could not fail to mark the difference in aspect between his dog and the two prizewinners.

One July morning both Lad and Bruce went through an hour of anguish. Both of them, one after the other, were plunged into a bathtub full of warm water and soap suds and were scrubbed right unmercifully. After which they were rubbed and curried and brushed for another hour until their coats shone resplendent. All day, at intervals, the brushing and combing were kept up.

Lad was indignant at such treatment, and he took no pains to hide his indignation. He knew perfectly well, from the undue attention, that a dog show was at hand. But not for a year or more had he himself been made ready for one. His lake baths and his thrice-a-week casual brushing at the mistress's hands had been, in that time, his only form of grooming. He had thought himself graduated forever from the nuisance of going to shows.

"What's the idea of dolling up old Laddie like that?" asked the Boy, as he came in for luncheon and found the mistress busy with comb and strap brush over the unhappy dog.

"For the Fourth of July Red Cross Dog Show at Ridgewood tomorrow," answered his mother, looking up, a little flushed, from her exertions.

"But I thought you and Dad said last year he was too old to show anymore," ventured the Boy.

"This time is different," said the mistress. "It's a specialty show, you see. And there is a cup offered for 'the best *veteran* dog of any recognized breed.' Isn't that fine? We didn't hear of the veteran cup till Dr. Hopper telephoned us about it this morning. So we're getting Lad ready. There *can't* be any other veteran as splendid as he is."

"No," agreed the Boy, dully, "I suppose not."

He went into the dining room, surreptitiously helped himself to a handful of lump sugar, and passed on out to the veranda. Wolf was sprawled, half asleep on the driveway lawn in the sun.

The dog's wolflike brush of tail began to thump against the shaven grass. Then, as the Boy stood on the veranda edge and snapped his fingers, Wolf got up from his soft resting place and started toward him, treading mincingly and with a sort of swagger, his slanting eyes half shut, his mouth a-grin.

"You know I've got sugar in my pocket as well as if you saw it," said the Boy. "Stop where you are."

Though the Boy accompanied his order with no gesture nor change of tone, the dog stopped dead a short ten feet away.

"Sugar is bad for dogs," went on the Boy. "It harms their teeth and their digestions. Didn't anybody ever tell you that, Wolfie?"

The dog's grin grew wider. His slanting eyes closed to mere glittering slits. He fidgeted a little, his tail fast wagging.

"But I guess a dog's got to have *some* kind of consolation prize when he can't go to a show," resumed the Boy. "Catch!"

As he spoke he suddenly drew a lump of sugar from his pocket, and, with the same motion, tossed it in the general direction of Wolf. Swift as was the Boy's action, Wolf's eye was still quicker. Springing high in air, the dog caught the flung cube of sugar as it flew above him and to one side. A second and a third lump were caught as deftly as the first.

Then the Boy took from his pocket the fourth and last lump. Descending the steps, he put his left hand across Wolf's eyes. With his right, he flipped the lump of sugar into a clump of shrubbery. "Find it!" he commanded, lifting the blindfold from the eyes of his pet.

Wolf darted hither and thither, stopped once or twice to sniff, then began to circle the nearer stretch of lawn, nose to ground. In less than two minutes he emerged from the shrubbery, placidly crunching the sugar lump between his mighty jaws.

"And yet they say you aren't fit to be shown!" exclaimed the Boy, fondling the dog's ears. "I'd give two years' growth if you could have a cup! You deserve one, all right; if only those judges had sense enough to study a collie's brain as well as the outside of his head!"

Wolf ran his nose into his master's cupped palm and whined. From the tone underlying the words he knew the Boy was unhappy, and he wanted to be of help.

The Boy went into the house again, to find his parents sitting down to lunch. Gathering his courage in both hands, he asked, "Is there going to be a novice class for collies, at Ridgewood, Dad?"

"Why, yes," said the master, "I suppose so. There always is."

"Do . . . do they give cups for the novice class?" inquired the Boy, with studied carelessness.

"Of course they don't," said the master, adding reminiscently, "though the first time we showed Lad, we put him in the novice class. And he won the blue ribbon there; so he had to go into the winners' class afterward. He got the winner's cup, you remember. So, indirectly, the novice class won him a cup."

"I see," said the Boy, not at all interested in this bit of ancient history. Then speaking very fast, he went on, "Well, a ribbon's better than nothing! Dad, will you do me a favor? Will you let me enter Wolfie for the novice class tomorrow? I'll pay the fee out of my allowance. Will you, Dad?"

The master looked at his son in blank amazement. Then he threw back his head and laughed loudly. The Boy flushed crimson and bit his lips.

"Why, dear!" hurriedly interposed the mistress, noting her son's discomfiture. "You wouldn't want Wolf to go there and be beaten by a lot of dogs that haven't half his brains or looks! It wouldn't be fair or kind to Wolf. He's so clever he'd know in a moment what was happening. He'd know he was beaten; nearly all dogs do. No, it wouldn't be fair to him."

"There's a 'mutt' class among the specials, Dr. Hopper says," put in the master, jocosely. "You might . . ."

"Wolf's *not* a mutt!" flashed the Boy, hotly. "He's no more of a mutt than Bruce or Lad, or Grey Mist, or Southport Sample, or any of the best ones. He has as good blood as all of them. Lad's his father, and Squire of Tytton was his grandfather, and Wishaw Clinker was his . . ."

"I'm sorry, Son," interposed the master, catching his wife's eye and dropping his tone of banter. "I apologize to you and to Wolf. He's not a 'mutt.' There's no better blood in colliedom than his, on both sides. But Mother is right. You'd only be putting him up to be beaten. And you wouldn't like that. He hasn't a single point that isn't hopelessly bad, from a judge's view. We've never taken a loser to a show from The Place. You don't want us to begin now, do you?"

"He has more brains than any dog alive except Lad!" declared the Boy, sullenly. "That ought to count."

"It ought to," agreed the mistress, soothingly. "And I wish it did. If it did, I know he'd win."

"It makes me sick to see a bushel of cups go to dogs that don't know enough to eat their own dinners," snorted the Boy. "I'm not talking about Lad and Bruce, but the thoroughbreds that are brought up in kennels and that have all their sense sacrificed for points. Why, Wolf's the cleverest— best—and he'll never even have one cup to show for it! He . . ."

He choked, and began to eat at top speed. The master and the mistress looked at each other and said nothing. They understood their son's chagrin as only a dog lover could. The mistress reached out and patted the Boy gently on the shoulder.

* * *

Next morning, directly after early breakfast, Lad and Bruce were put into the tonneau of the car. The mistress and the master and the Boy climbed in, and the twelve-mile journey to Ridgewood began.

Wolf, left to guard The Place, watched the departing show goers until the car turned out of the gate, a furlong above. Then, with a sigh, he curled up on a porch mat, his nose between his snowy little paws, and prepared for a day of loneliness.

The Red Cross dog show, that Fourth of July, was a triumph for The Place.

Bruce won ribbon after ribbon in the collie division, easily taking "winners" at the last, and thus adding another gorgeous silver cup to his collection. Then, when the supreme event of the day—"Best dog in the show"—was called, and the winners of each breed were led into the ring, the judges scanned and handled the group of sixteen for barely five minutes before awarding to Bruce the dark blue rosette and the "Best Dog" cup.

The crowd around the ring's railing applauded loudly. But they applauded still more loudly a little later, when, after a brief survey of six aged thoroughbreds, the judge pointed to Lad, who was standing like a mahogany statue at one end of the ring.

These six dogs had all been famed prize winners in their time. And above all the rest, Lad was adjudged worthy of the "veteran" cup. There was a haze of happy tears in the mistress's eyes as she led him from the ring. It seemed a beautiful climax for his grand old life. She wiped her eyes, unashamed, whispering praise the while to her stately dog.

It was a celebration evening for the two prize dogs when they got home. But everybody was tired from the day's events, and by ten o'clock the house was dark. Wolf, on his veranda mat, alone of all The Place's denizens, was awake.

Vaguely Wolf knew the other dogs had done some praiseworthy thing. He would have known it, if for no other reason, from the remorseful hug the Boy had given him before going to bed.

Well, some must win honors and petting and the right to sleep indoors while others must plod along at the only work they are fit for, and must sleep out in thunderstorm or clear, in heat or freezing cold. That was life. Being only a dog, Wolf was too wise to complain of life and took things as he found them, making the very best of his share.

He snoozed, now, in the warm darkness. Two hours later he got up, stretched himself lazily fore and aft, collie-fashion, and trotted forth for the night's first patrol of the grounds.

A few minutes afterward he was skirting the lake edge at the foot of the lawn, a hundred yards below the house. The night was pitch dark, except for pulses of heat lightning, now and then, far to westward. Half a mile out on the lake two men in an anchored scow were cat fishing.

A small skiff was slipping along very slowly, not fifty feet offshore.

Wolf did not give the skiff a second glance. Boats were no novelty to him, nor did they interest him in the least—except when they showed signs of running ashore somewhere along his beat.

This skiff was not headed for land, but was paralleling the shore. It crept along at a snail's pace and in dead silence. A man, its only occupant, sat at the oars, scarcely moving them as he kept his boat in motion.

A dog is ridiculously nearsighted, more so than almost any other beast. Keen hearing and keener scent are its chief guides. At three-hundred yards' distance it cannot, by eye, recognize its master, nor tell him from a stranger. But at close quarters, even in the darkest night, a dog's vision is far more piercing and accurate than man's under like conditions.

Wolf thus saw the skiff and its occupant while he himself was still invisible. The boat was no concern of his. So he trotted on to the far end of The Place, where the forest joined the orchard.

On his return tour of the lake edge he saw the skiff again. It had shifted its direction and was now barely ten feet offshore—so near to the bank that one of the oars occasionally grated on the pebbly bottom. The oarsman was looking intently toward the house.

Wolf paused, uncertain. The average watchdog, his attention thus attracted, would have barked. But Wolf knew the lake was public property. Boats were often rowed as close to shore as this without intent to trespass. It was not the skiff that caught Wolf's attention as he paused there on the brink, it was the man's furtive scrutiny of the house.

A pale flare of heat lightning turned the world momentarily from jet black to a dim sulfur color. The boatman saw Wolf standing, alert and suspicious, among the lakeside grasses, not ten feet away. He started slightly, and a soft, throaty growl from the dog answered him.

The man seemed to take the growl as a challenge—and to accept it. He reached into his pocket and drew something out. When the next faint glow of lightning illumined the shore, the man lifted the thing he had taken from his pocket and hurled it at Wolf.

With all the incredible swiftness bred in his wolf ancestry, the dog shrank to one side, readily dodging the missile, which struck the lawn just behind him. Teeth bared in a ferocious snarl, Wolf dashed forward through the shallow water toward the skiff.

But the man apparently had had enough of the business. He rowed off with long strokes into deep water. And once there, he kept on rowing until distance and darkness hid him.

Wolf stood, chest deep in water, listening to the far-off oar strokes until they died away. He was not fool enough to swim in pursuit, well knowing that a swimming dog is worse than helpless against a boatman.

Moreover, the intruder had been scared away. That was all that concerned Wolf. He turned back to shore. His vigil was ended for another few hours. It was time to take up his nap where he had left it off.

Before he had taken two steps, his sensitive nostrils were full of the scent of raw meat. There, on the lawn ahead of him, lay a chunk of beef as big as a fist. This, then, was what the boatman had thrown at him.

Wolf pricked up his ears in appreciation, and his brush began to vibrate. Trespassers had once or twice tried to stone him. But this was the first time any of them had pelted him with delicious raw beef. Evidently, Lad and Bruce were not the only collies on The Place to receive prizes that day.

Wolf stooped over the meat, sniffed at it, then caught it up between his jaws.

Now, a dog is the easiest animal alive to poison, just as a cat is the hardest. For a dog will usually bolt a mouthful of poisoned meat without pausing to chew or otherwise investigate it. A cat, on the contrary, smells

←——————————————————————————————————→

and tastes everything first and chews it scientifically before swallowing it. The slightest unfamiliar scent or flavor warns her to sheer off from the feast.

So the average dog would have gulped this toothsome windfall in a single swallow. But Wolf was not the average dog. No collie is. And Wolf was still more like his eccentric forefathers of the wilderness than are most collies.

He lacked the reasoning powers to make him suspicious of this rich gift from a stranger. But a queer personal trait now served him just as well.

Wolf was an epicure. He always took three times as long to empty his dinner dish as did the other dogs. For instead of gobbling his meal, as they did, he was wont to nibble affectedly at each morsel, gnawing it slowly into nothingness, all the time showing a fussily dainty relish of it that used to delight the Boy and send guests into peals of laughter.

This odd little trait that had caused so much ridicule now saved Wolf's life.

He carried the lump of beef gingerly up to the veranda, laid it down on his mat, and prepared to revel in his chance banquet after his own deliberate fashion.

Holding the beef between his forepaws, he proceeded to devour it in mincing little squirrel bites. About a quarter of the meat had disappeared when Wolf became aware that his tongue smarted and that his throat was sore. Also that the interior of the meat ball had a rankly pungent odor, very different from the delicious fragrance of its outside and not at all appetizing.

He looked down at the chunk, rolled it over with his nose, surveyed it again, then got up and moved away from it in angry disgust.

Presently he forgot his disappointment in the knowledge that he was very, very ill. His tongue and throat no longer burned, but his body and brain seemed full of hot lead that weighed a ton. He felt stupid and too weak to stir. A great drowsiness gripped him.

With a grunt of discomfort and utter fatigue, he slumped down on the veranda floor to sleep off his sick lassitude. After that, for a time, nothing mattered.

For perhaps an hour Wolf lay sprawling there, dead to his duty and to everything else. Then faintly, through the fog of dullness that enwrapped his brain, came a sound—a sound he had long ago learned to listen for. The harshly scraping noise of a boat's prow drawn up on the pebbly shore at the foot of the lawn.

Instinct tore through the poison vapors and roused the sick dog. He lifted his head. It was strangely heavy and hard to lift.

The sound was repeated as the prow was pulled farther up on the bank. Then came the crunch of a human foot on the waterside grass.

Heredity and training and lifelong fidelity took control of the lethargic dog, dragging him to his feet and down the veranda steps through no volition of his own.

Every move tired him. He was dizzy and nauseated. He craved sleep. But as he was just a thoroughbred dog and not a wise human, he did not stop to think up good reason why he should neglect his duty because he did not feel like performing it.

To the brow of the hill he trotted—slowly, heavily, shakily. His sharp powers of hearing told him the trespasser had left his boat and had taken one or two stealthy steps up the slope of lawn toward the house.

And now a puff of west wind brought Wolf's sense of smell into action. A dog remembers odors as humans remember faces. And the breeze bore to him the scent of the same man who had flung ashore that bit of meat that had caused all his suffering.

He had caught the man's scent an hour earlier, as he had stood sniffing at the boat ten feet away from him. The same scent had been on the meat the man had handled.

And now, having played such a cruel trick on him, the joker was actually daring to intrude on The Place!

A gust of resentful rage pierced the dullness of Wolf's brain and sent a thrill of fierce energy through him. For the moment this carried him out of his sick self and brought back all his former zest as a watchdog.

Down the hill, like a furry whirlwind, flew Wolf, every tooth bared, his back abristle from neck to tail. Now he was well within sight of the intruder. He saw the man pausing to adjust something to one of his hands. Then, before this could be accomplished, Wolf saw him pause and stare through the darkness as the wild onrush of the dog's feet struck upon his hearing.

Another instant—and Wolf was near enough to spring. Out of the blackness he launched himself, straight for the trespasser's throat. The man saw the dim shape hurtling through the air toward him. He dropped what he was carrying and flung up both hands to guard his neck. At that, he was none too soon. For just as the thief's palm reached his own throat, Wolf's teeth met in the fleshy part of the hand.

Silent, in agony, the man beat at the dog with his free hand. But an attacking collie is hard to locate in the darkness. A bulldog will secure a grip and will hang on. A collie is everywhere at once.

Wolf's snapping jaws had already deserted the robber's mangled hand and slashed the man's left shoulder to the bone. Then the dog made another furious lunge for the throat.

Down crashed the man, losing his balance under the heavy impact, Wolf atop of him. To guard his throat, the man rolled over on his face, kicking madly at the dog and reaching back for his own hip-pocket. Half in the water and half on the bank, the two rolled and thrashed and struggled—the man panting and wheezing in mortal terror; the dog growling in a hideous, snarling fashion as might a wild animal.

The thief's torn left hand found a grip on Wolf's fur-armored throat. He shoved the fiercely writhing dog backward, jammed a pistol against Wolf's head, and pulled the trigger!

The dog relaxed his grip and tumbled in a huddled heap on the brink. The man staggered, gasping, to his feet—bleeding, disheveled, his clothes torn and mud coated.

The echoes of the shot were still reverberating among the lakeside hills. Several of the house's dark windows leaped into sudden light—then more windows in another room—and in another.

The thief swore roundly. His night's work was ruined. He turned to his skiff and shoved it into the water. Then he turned to grope for what he had dropped on the lawn when Wolf's unexpected attack had interfered with his plans.

As he did so, something seized him by the ankle. In panic the man screamed aloud and jumped into the water. Then, peering back, he saw what happened.

Wolf, sprawling and unable to stand, had reached forward from where he lay and had driven his teeth for the last time into his foe.

The thief raised his pistol again and fired in the general direction of the prostrate dog. Then he clambered into his boat and rowed off with frantic speed, just as a salvo of barks told him that Lad and Bruce had been released from the house. They came charging down the lawn, the master at their heels.

But already the quick oar beats were growing distant, and the gloom had blotted out any chance of seeing or following the boat.

Wolf lay on his side, half in and half out of the water. He could not rise, as was his custom, to meet the Boy, who came running up, close behind the master and valorously grasping a target rifle. But the dog wagged his tail in feeble greeting. Then he looked out over the black lake and snarled.

The bullet had grazed Wolf's scalp and then had passed along the foreleg, scarring and numbing it. But no damage had been done that a week's good nursing would not set right.

The marks in the grass and the poisoned meat on the porch told their own tale. So did the neat kit of burglar tools and a rubber glove found near the foot of the lawn. And then the telephone was put to work.

At dawn, a man in torn and muddy clothes called at the office of a doctor three miles away to be treated for a half-dozen dog bites received, he said, from a pack of stray curs he had met on the turnpike. By the time his wounds were dressed, the sheriff and two deputies had arrived to take him in charge. In his pockets were a revolver, with two cartridges fired, and the mate of the rubber glove he had left on The Place's lawn.

* * *

←——————————————————————————————————→

"You—you wouldn't let Wolfie go to any show and win a cup for himself," half sobbed the Boy, as the master worked over the injured dog's wound, "but he's saved you from losing all the cups the other dogs ever won!"

Three days later the master came home from a trip to the city. He went directly to the Boy's room. There on a rug lounged the convalescent Wolf, the Boy sitting beside him, stroking the dog's bandaged head.

"Wolf," said the master, solemnly, "I've been talking about you to some people I know. And we all agree . . ."

He paused.

"Agree *what?*" asked the Boy, looking up in mild curiosity.

The master cleared his throat and continued, "We agree that the trophy shelf in my study hasn't enough cups on it. So I've decided to add still another to the collection. Want to see it, Son?"

From behind his back the master produced a gleaming silver cup—one of the largest and most ornate the Boy had ever seen, larger even than Bruce's "Best Dog" cup.

The Boy took it from his father's outstretched hand.

"Who won this?" he asked. "And what for? Didn't we get all the cups that were coming to us at the shows? Is it . . .?"

The Boy's voice trailed away into a gurgle of bewildered rapture. He had caught sight of the lettering on the big cup. And now, his arm around Wolf, he read the inscription aloud, stammering with delight as he blurted out the words: **"HERO CUP. WON BY WOLF AGAINST ALL COMERS."**

* * * * *

"Wolf," by Albert Payson Terhune. Published April 1919 in *St. Nicholas*. Albert Payson Terhune (1872–1942) lived all his life in New Jersey. He was on the staff of the *New York Evening World*, from 1896 to 1916, and was one of the most popular authors of his time, writing hundreds of articles and short stories (mostly having to do with dogs) and around forty books.

Delayed Delivery

Cathy Miller

"Christmas alone" . . . perhaps as bleak a two-word image as exists in the English language. It is hard enough to face Christmas alone if one has become somewhat inured to the anguish with the passing of the years. It is something else again if your life partner is suddenly taken from you—the sweetheart who, over the years, meshed into oneness with you. This is the sorrow America's greatest poetess, Emily Dickinson, was thinking of when she wrote,

> *The sweeping up the Heart, And putting Love away*
> *We shall not want to use again, Until Eternity.*

A Canadian teacher and freelance writer responded to a 1992 Christmas story contest in her area newspaper, Northern Life. *Her story won first prize. Mrs. Maimu Veedler, of Lively, Ontario, was given a copy of my book,* Christmas in my Heart, *and responding to a call for extra-special stories, sent me a copy of this prizewinning narrative. I called the genial editor, Ms. Carol Mulligan, who in turn contacted Mrs. Miller of Sudbury, Ontario. Mrs. Miller called me—and permission was granted to include her moving story of a delayed gift that arrived at just the right time.*

* * * * *

There had never been a winter like this. Stella watched from the haven of her armchair as gusts of snow whipped themselves into a frenzy. The houses across the street were all but obliterated by the fury of wind-blown flakes.

Dragging her gaze from the window, she forced herself up out of her chair and waited a moment for balance to reassert itself. Straightening her back against the pain that threatened to keep her stooped, she set out determinedly for the kitchen.

In the doorway to the next room she paused, her mind blank, wondering what purpose had propelled her there. From the vent above the stove, the scream of the wind threatened to funnel the afternoon storm directly down into the tiny house. Stella focused brown eyes on the stove-top clock. The three-fifteen time reminded her that she had headed in there to take something out of the freezer for her supper. Another lonely meal that she didn't feel like preparing, much less eating.

Suddenly, she grabbed the handle of the refrigerator and leaned her forehead against the cold, white surface of the door as a wave of self-pity threatened to drown her. It was too much to bear, losing her beloved Dave this summer! How was she to endure the pain, the daily nothingness? She felt the familiar ache in her throat and squeezed her eyes tightly shut to hold the tears at bay.

Stella had known that Dave wouldn't live to see Christmas. When the doctors had diagnosed her husband's terminal cancer last January, her world had shattered. But through the ensuing months Dave had managed to put his affairs in order, to show her everything she needed to learn about managing the house—everything except how to live without him. Now the loneliness weighed upon her like lethargy, stealing her energy, her ability to find joy in life, even in Christmas.

She had turned down an invitation to spend the holiday with old friends in Florida. Somehow that had seemed worse than staying home alone. Not only would she miss her husband of forty-eight years, but she would miss the snow and the familiarity of home. They had been a childless couple and in the last decade had lost several friends and even family. But it had been all bearable with Dave by her side. Bearable until now.

"Oh, Dave, I miss you so!" The sound of her own voice echoed hollowly in the room. She turned on the radio that sat on the counter next to a neatly descending row of wooden canisters. A sudden, joyful chorus of Christmas music served only to deepen her loneliness. With shaky fingers she lowered the volume to a muted background.

She was surprised by the slap of damp envelopes on the floor as the mailman dropped them through the door slot. With the inevitable wince of pain, she bent to retrieve them. Moving to the living room, she sat on the piano bench and opened them. They were mostly Christmas cards, and her sad eyes smiled at the traditional scenes and the loving messages inside. Carefully, her arthritic fingers arranged them among the others clustered on the piano top. In her entire house, they were the only seasonal decoration. Christmas was only days away, but she just didn't have the heart to put up a tree or bring out the stable that Dave had lovingly built.

Suddenly engulfed by the finality of her aloneness, Stella buried her lined face in her hands, lowering her elbows to the piano keys in an abrasive discord, and let the tears come. How would she get through Christmas and the dismal winter months beyond? She longed to climb into bed and bury herself in a cocoon of blankets, not emerging until her friends and spring returned.

The ring of the doorbell startled her. Who could be calling on such a stormy afternoon? The doorbell sounded a second time. Wiping her eyes, she pulled herself off the bench to answer it.

She opened the wooden door and stared through the screened window of the storm door with consternation. On her front porch, buffeted by waves of wind and snow, stood a young man, his hatless head barely visible above the large carton in his arms. She peered beyond him to the driveway, but there was nothing about the small car to give a clue to his identity. Returning her gaze to him, she saw that his hands were bare and his eyebrows had lifted in an expression of hopeful appeal that was fast disappearing behind the frost forming on the glass. Summoning courage, the elderly lady opened the door slightly, and he stepped sideways to speak into the space.

"Mrs. Thornhope?"

Stella nodded, her extended arm beginning to tremble with cold and the strain of holding the door against the wind.

"I have a package for you."

Curiosity won over caution. She pushed the door enough for the stranger to shoulder it open and stepped back into the foyer to make room. He entered, bringing with him the frozen breath of the storm. Smiling, he carefully placed his burden on the floor, then handed her the envelope that protruded from an inner jacket pocket. Suddenly, a muffled yelp came from the box. Stella actually jumped. The man laughed and bent to straighten up the cardboard flaps wide enough for her to peek inside.

It was a dog! A golden Labrador retriever puppy, to be exact. As the young man lifted its squirming body up into his arms, he explained, "This is for you, ma'am. He's six weeks old and completely housebroken." The young pup wiggled in happiness at being released from captivity and thrust ecstatic kisses in the direction of the young man's face. "We were supposed to deliver him on Christmas Eve," he continued with some difficulty, trying to raise his chin out of reach, "but the staff at the kennels start their holidays tomorrow. Hope you don't mind an early present."

Shock had stolen her ability to think clearly. Unable to form coherent sentences, she stammered, "But . . . I don't . . . I mean . . . who . . .?

The young fellow set the animal down on the doormat between them and then reached out a finger to tap the envelope in her fingers. "The letter pretty much explains everything. The dog was bought last July while his mother was still pregnant. It was meant to be a Christmas gift. I have some other things in the car. I'll get them."

Before she could protest, he disappeared back into the snowstorm. He returned carrying another big box with a leash, dog food, and a book entitled *Caring for Your Labrador Retriever*. All this time the puppy had sat quietly at her feet, panting happily as his brown eyes watched her.

Unbelievably, the stranger was turning to go. Desperation forced the words from her lips. "But who . . . who bought it?"

Pausing in the open doorway, his words almost snatched away by the wind, he replied, "Your husband ma'am." And then he was gone.

It was all in the letter. Forgetting the puppy entirely at the sight of the familiar handwriting, Stella walked like a sleepwalker to her armchair by the window. Unaware that the little dog had followed her, she forced tear-filled eyes to read her husband's words. He had written it three weeks before his death and had left it with the kennel owners to be delivered with the puppy as his last gift to her.

Dear Stella,

Of all the letters I've written you, this has to be the hardest. How do I put into words all the things I feel for you? Sometimes I wish you could be me—live inside my head and heart, just for a day. Then you'd know how much I love you. You've been the best wife a man could ask for, my lover and my best friend. I know how hard this cancer's been on you. I don't know where you get the strength to take care of me like you do and never complain. Your smile is the first thing I see every morning, and your gentle voice is the last thing I hear at night as you read to me or sing me to sleep. I couldn't ask for a better nurse. The time may come when I'll have to move to the hospital, but it's been wonderful to stay here in our home with you for this long.

You're a strong woman, Stella. I know if you're reading this letter it means I'm gone. But don't be afraid. I've been gone before, on my trips with work, and you've managed fine without me. Just think of this as one of my trips. It won't be forever. You'll be joining me someday. We both believe that! I know you'll be lonely, so I'm sending you this pup to keep you company. His mother reminded me of the dog we had when I was a kid—Daisy Mae. She was a wonderful companion, as I hope this little fellow will be for you.

It will be winter as you read this. People say we "older folks" are in our winter years. But I've never even felt like autumn with you, Stella. It's always been spring for us, hasn't it? I have a feeling that where I'm going it'll be spring again.

I'll wait for you there.

Love, Dave

Remembering the puppy for the first time, Stella was surprised to find him patiently looking at her, his small panting mouth resembling a comic smile. She put the pages aside and reached for the bundle of golden fur. She had thought he would be heavier, but he weighed no more than a sofa pillow. And so soft and warm! She cradled him in her arms, and he licked her jaw, then snuggled into the hollow of her neck. The tears began again at this exchange of affection, and the dog endured her crying without moving.

Finally, Stella lowered him to her lap where he regarded her solemnly. She wiped vaguely at her wet cheeks, then mustered a smile.

"Well, little guy, I guess it's you and me." His pink tongue panted in agreement. Stella's smile strengthened, and her gaze shifted sideways to the window. Dusk had fallen, and the storm seemed to have spent the worst of its fury. Through fluffy flakes that were now drifting down at a gentler pace, she saw the cheery Christmas lights that edged the roof lines of her neighbors' homes. The strains of "Joy to the World" wafted in from the kitchen.

Suddenly Stella felt the most amazing sensation of peace and benediction washing over her. It was like being enfolded in a loving embrace. Her heart beat painfully, but it was with joy and wonder, not grief or loneliness.

Rising from her chair, she spoke to the little dog whose ears perked up at the sound of her voice. "You know, fella, I have a box in the basement that I think you'd like. There's a tree in it and some decorations and lights that will impress you like crazy. And I think I can find that old stable down there too. What do you say we go hunt it up?"

The puppy barked happily in agreement, as if he understood every word.

* * * * *

His Adopted Friend

Abbie Farwell Brown

To Harvey Rich, it was the greatest temptation of his life, and he gave in to it. And he was happy. Sort of. Then came a long, long night during which he could not sleep. The next morning, he knew what he must do.

* * * * *

It was a small country circus of the cheap and ordinary kind which occasionally stopped at Farmtown, but to Harvey Rich it seemed the finest and most remarkable of shows. It was not, however, the clowns nor the fancy riding on the beautiful horses, the acrobats nor the human freaks which he watched so eagerly, though he enjoyed them also. But the center of attraction to him was Monsieur Pinaud's troupe of trained dogs, and he went fairly wild over their performance.

Harvey had always been very fond of dogs, and had hoped that some day he might own a fine, large one himself. But he and his mother were too poor now to buy such a dog as he wanted, and the day seemed very far away. Meanwhile he made friends with every dog for miles around and studied all about them in books until he became known both in the village and outside as quite an authority upon the subject. Many a sick puppy had Harvey tended and cured, adding quite a few dollars to his earnings by his modest "doctor's bills."

They were a fine troupe of dogs and did their tricks well. But from the first Harvey singled out one particular dog and kept his eyes upon him alone in breathless interest. This was a splendid great mastiff, Caesar, the leader of the band and the most intelligent of them all.

When the show was over, Harvey went home with a glowing account of the performance for his mother and a feeling that at last he had found just the dog he had always wanted. Oh, if only he could have a dog like Caesar! All that afternoon he puzzled and planned how he could earn a lot of money to buy him. But then, he thought, hopelessly, *even if I could buy him they probably wouldn't sell him for any amount of money.*

It was late that night, after the evening performance, and Harvey was tossing sleeplessly in bed, still thinking of Caesar, when there came a knock at the front door, and dressing himself hastily, he went down to open it.

One of the neighbors, Jim Trask, stood there with a strange man and a wheelbarrow on which was something dark.

"Hello, Harvey!" said Jim. "This is Mr. Pinaud, of the circus. Some mean fellow shot this big mastiff just now, an' I told him to come to you, seein' you know more 'bout dogs than other folks, an' cured my dog when he got shot last spring."

Harvey's heart gave a bound, and he was soon on his knees beside the wheelbarrow.

"Oh, poor fellow!" he said, soothingly, and Caesar stopped whining to lick his hand. Trembling with eagerness, Harvey lighted a lamp and examined the dog.

"We go away very soon—quite now," spoke up the Frenchman, anxiously. "Very hard to carry sick dog. Caesar my best show dog—I cannot afford to lose. You tell me, is he for to die?"

Harvey's fingers trembled as he bent over the dog again. It was not a very serious wound, he thought, and he was quite sure he could cure it if he had time. But now they would take Caesar away, and perhaps he might die on the road.

"He is badly hurt," Harvey said at last, in a low tone.

The Frenchman sighed. "Poor fellow! If he cannot get well, I leave him." Harvey started at the words. "I hate to have him kill. But if he suffer, I tell you to kill him. I leave him here; I cannot do it. You sure he not get well?"

Harvey had been struggling with a great temptation. He hesitated.

"I don't think . . . he can possibly get well," he said at last, in a hoarse, strained voice. "If you take him tonight, he will certainly die."

The Frenchman gave a sob; he was very thin and hollow-cheeked, and seemed sick himself.

"Adieu," he said, bending affectionately over the dog and kissing the noble forehead twice. "Good dog!" Then he turned to Harvey, his lips trembling. "I must now to go," he said, brokenly. "You not let him to suffer? Have him shot quick?" Then he rose and hurried away.

Harvey carried Caesar tenderly into the house, made a bed for him by the fire, and began to dress the wound. The bullet had gone quite through his leg, and the poor dog suffered badly, but he was very patient under Harvey's touch. The boy worked over him nervously.

He sat up with the dog all night, and the firm affection between the two dated from that time. For in a few weeks Caesar got well and became the boy's constant friend and companion. Mrs. Rich had received the dog doubtfully at first, he was so huge and ate so much. But she soon grew to love him almost as well as Harvey.

The boy's conscience troubled him now and then when he thought how he had deceived Caesar's master, but only Jim Trask had heard what was said, and no one, not even Jim, knew that Harvey had been sure of the dog's recovery from the first. Everyone congratulated him on his luck in saving the dog, and thought he must be a very fine doctor. Indeed, Harvey was treated with new respect, both on account of his reputation as a surgeon and on Caesar's account, for the latter now became a universal favorite.

Summer came around again, and Caesar had been with him nearly a year. Harvey had finished school now and was looking for a position, which in this little country town was not easy to find. But there were many summer boarders in Farmtown, and Harvey earned considerable money from them by doing chores and errands or acting as guide and boatman on the river. When they found out Caesar's accomplishments he, too, had a chance to earn money for his master, for it became quite the fashion to give little afternoon teas and lawn parties at which Harvey Rich and his trick-dog were the chief attraction. Among the children, especially, Caesar became a great favorite, and he was as fond of them.

Among the cottagers to take a special interest in Caesar and his master was Mr. Conant, a wealthy dry goods merchant from the city of Boston. His little daughter, Grace, had grown very fond of the big dog and insisted on going to see him every day or having him come to her. And so the three of them became great friends.

One morning toward the end of the summer Mr. Conant called at the Rich cottage and offered to buy Caesar for his daughter.

Harvey turned white and looked as if he had been struck.

"Sell Caesar!" he gasped. "Sell my Caesar! Oh, Mr. Conant, I couldn't do it!"

Mr. Conant reasoned with him in vain, raising his offer until he stopped finally at five hundred dollars [about $20,000 in today's money].

"You would be a foolish boy to refuse that," he said, sharply, for he began to consider Harvey very obstinate and selfishly disregarding of his mother's needs as well as of his own.

Harvey bit his lip. "I can't take it, Sir," he said, desperately. "I can't give up the dog to anyone—not for any money. You don't understand, Sir. I *can't* do it, and that's all there is about it."

Harvey dared not look up, but he felt Mr. Conant's sharp eyes upon him and heard his sniff of surprise as he turned to go.

"I am much disappointed," he said. "Good-morning."

Harvey went miserably into the house, feeling that he had lost a friend and the chances of further engagements with Caesar. But worst of all was his new sense of guilt, which now tinged even his affection for the dog with a feeling of shame.

A week went by without the customary mornings at the Evergreens' or calls from Grace and her nurse, which both Harvey and Caesar sadly missed. Then came one morning when the town was covered with flaming placards announcing the arrival of Monsieur Pinaud's circus company.

Harvey caught sight of one of these when he went to the store, and he could hardly believe his eyes. He had never thought of their coming back! It was with very different feelings from those of last year that he now glanced over the highly colored posters. With a sinking heart he slunk guiltily home, and all day he kept Caesar chained in the barn, hardly daring to go out himself lest he should meet some of the circus people who might inquire about Caesar. He behaved so strangely that his mother was much worried about him and watched him anxiously. At night he stole away and was gone quite late, so that at last she went to bed without seeing him, but listened anxiously for his return. He had gone to the circus; it was impossible to stay away.

Harvey sat unmoved through the first part of the performance, and only when the trained dogs came in did he flush and turn uneasily on his seat.

They were a pitiful little troupe—quite commonplace and uninteresting without Caesar to lead them. There was little enthusiasm over them, and their trainer, a woman in a red riding-habit, seemed sad and discouraged. *But where is Monsieur Pinaud?* Harvey wondered with a guilty feeling, remembering his hollow chest and feeble voice.

After the performance, he lingered uneasily until the faded little woman re-entered the tent for her whip, which she had forgotten. Harvey went up to her timidly.

"Monsieur Pinaud?" he said, inquiringly, "Isn't he here this year?

"Oh, yes," she answered, listlessly. "He owns the show, you know. I'm his wife. But he's sick now and can't do much of anything but count the money." Her face grew worried.

"Is he very sick?" asked Harvey quickly.

"The doctor said—the last one we could afford to have—that he couldn't live but a few weeks. He's been on the decline for a long time now. It most broke his heart losing Caesar, his best dog, a year ago. It was right in this town. We've had bad luck ever since."

Harvey hesitated and looked after her wistfully. Then slowly and with a heavy load on his heart he went home, all his pleasure in owning Caesar gone. He crept miserably into bed, and all night long he tossed and turned, unable to sleep. He was haunted by Monsieur Pinaud's thin cheeks and hollow eyes as he had last seen them. He went over it all from the beginning, over and over again, and every time he saw himself in a meaner light. He had stolen a dog—he realized it at last—and he felt unworthy to be a dog's master; such a noble animal as Caesar was, too, and he poor and weak and miserable!

In the morning, Harvey woke to find his mother bending anxiously over him. Then brokenly, but with a firm purpose to confess his fault as a first step toward atoning for it, he told her everything and asked what he should do next. The circus had gone away that night, and Harvey did not know where. His mother was very sympathetic and eager to help him, though she, too, was heartbroken at the thought of parting with Caesar. Then they thought of Mr. Conant, and Harvey resolved to go to him because he had always shown such interest in the dog, though he dreaded the confession which he had to make.

Mr. Conant received him rather coldly.

"Well," he said sharply, "have you reconsidered your refusal to sell Caesar? Or are you still as obstinate as ever?"

"I can't sell Caesar, Mr. Conant," said Harvey, bravely, "because he doesn't belong to me. I am going to give him back."

Then hurriedly Harvey confessed the whole story, omitting nothing and not trying to excuse himself at all. Mr. Conant listened in silence, with increasing interest and kindliness on his face. At last Harvey finished, and then, pulling out a little purse, he handed it to Mr. Conant, saying timidly, "It isn't much, but it is all I have saved up this last year toward a bicycle. Caesar helped to earn it, and I want Monsieur Pinaud to have that, too, to help repay him for what I made him lose."

Mr. Conant laid his hand affectionately on the boy's shoulder.

"I am very glad you told me," he said, heartily, "more glad than I can say. Harvey, you are a good fellow, and I am proud of you. But I am sorry we must lose Caesar."

Harvey's lip trembled, and noticing it Mr. Conant went on to plan the finding of Monsieur Pinaud.

"I see by the paper that the company is in Boston now," he said. "I am going up there myself tonight, to open our house and get it ready for the family to come home next week, and I will take Caesar up with me and give him to Monsieur Pinaud myself, if I can find him."

Harvey gratefully agreed to this, and so it was settled. He took leave of Mr. Conant with a hearty handshake, then he paused, and his face fell.

"I . . . I have said Goodbye to Caesar," he said, trying to be cheerful. "I guess I won't see him again. If you would be so kind as to send someone after him, with Gracie; he will go with her without any fuss."

Harvey tried to be brave. He had done wrong and was now doing his best to make up for it. But it was very hard. No one but his mother knew how hard.

It was toward evening on the third day after he had lost Caesar when he received a message that he was wanted at the Evergreens'. Anxious to hear the latest news from his friend, Harvey hastened to the cottage. The family were gathered on the lawn and greeted him kindly.

"Well, Harvey," said Mr. Conant, gravely, "I found the circus troupe and gave Caesar back to Monsieur Pinaud. It was just in time to give the poor man a last great pleasure."

Harvey turned pale. "Is he dead?" he asked, quickly.

Mr. Conant bowed his head. "He had been ill for several years with consumption and could not possibly get well. You have nothing to reproach yourself with on that account, my boy," he said, earnestly. "He would have died at this time, anyway. You can imagine how pleased and grateful he was to receive Caesar back again. He insisted that he owed you a great deal of money for saving the dog and would not hear to taking your money. And that night when he died his last words were, 'Give Caesar to the good boy who saved his life.' "

Harvey's face flushed with shame. "I didn't deserve to have him think so of me," he burst out, impetuously.

"Perhaps not. But he was so happy in the thought that I could not bear to contradict him. Still, Mrs. Pinaud is very poor, and it was not right that she should lose Caesar without receiving something for him. But the circus company is to break up now, and she was only too glad to sell Caesar. Putting the money you gave me with some more, I bought Caesar for the price which you refused from me, Harvey."

Harvey's face was lowered, and his lips trembled. So Mr. Conant was to have Caesar after all, and he should never see him again, probably. It was very hard, but he knew that it was no more than he deserved.

"It is too bad," said Mr. Conant. "Of course, I meant to buy the dog for you, Harvey, and take you both up to the city where you could have a good position in my store and where Grace could see Caesar often.

"You and your mother must come up to the city, anyway, if you will," Mr. Conant went on, earnestly. "We shall be very glad to do all we can to help you. But I am sorry about Caesar. I am afraid we shall have to get along without him somehow."

Harvey looked up quickly. "Oh! Has anything happened to him?" he asked, anxiously.

"The very night when Monsieur Pinaud died, Caesar disappeared, and we can find no trace of him high or low. We think that someone stole him."

It was a second blow for Harvey, and at first he was too much dazed to think. He felt weak and sick and faint, and thought he was going to fall.

Just at this moment, as if he had planned it all for a most effective entrance, there was a scuffle in the hedge, a loud bark of joy, and before Harvey knew what had happened, two huge paws were resting on his shoulders and a big red tongue was covering his face with kisses! It was Caesar, mud-stained and dirty! He had evidently run away and come back all these fifty miles to Harvey. Not finding him at his own home, he had followed his trail to the Evergreens and was now assisting in the jolliest reunion ever seen on the little lawn.

Half crazy with joy, Harvey hugged his dog—now his very own for good and always—leaving off only to run and shake hands gratefully with Mr. Conant, who stood by laughing at the excitement, then dancing around with Grace and Caesar until they were all three tired and out of breath. Then Mr. Conant seized the chance of speaking a word.

"Well, my boy," he said, "you have had your lesson and your punishment. You will have to go without your bicycle. But I think you would rather have your dog. Now, will you accept my offer this time? Will you and Caesar come up to the city with us next week?"

They both gladly agreed that they would, and Caesar and his friend came to the city and saw and conquered.

* * * * *

"His Adopted Friend," by Abbie Farwell Brown. Published September 1897 in the *Woman's Home Companion*. Abbie Farwell Brown (1881–1927) was born in Boston to a "blue-blooded" family whose American roots dated back to the *Mayflower*. After studying at Radcliffe, she went on to author such beloved books as *The Lonesomest Doll, The Christmas Angel, The Heart of New England,* and *The Silver Stair*. She is considered to be one of the leading writers of children's prose and poetry for the turn of the twentieth century.

Scottie Scores a Triumph

John Scott Douglas

Davis Andrews wanted to be free of entanglements. Be they job, location, or woman, he wanted none of them to tie him down. So he left them all and hit the road. Ah! Free at last!

But along the way, a strange thing happened—a very small, dark, strange thing.

* * * * *

Davis Andrews was broiling his chops over a bed of red coals in a grove south of Birmingham, Alabama, when he caught sight of a Scotch terrier. The little black dog was walking across the deserted grove in a dignified manner, his sagebrush of a tail held straight up and waving slightly as he walked.

It's miles from any dwelling, was the young man's thought. *The little fellow's wandered away while someone was camping here, and was left behind.* . . . "Come here, Scottie."

The little dog lost his dignity in a flash, and he came bounding toward the big, roughhewn youth, his tail wagging vigorously. Davis scratched the friendly little animal's ears for a moment and then turned back to his sizzling chops. Scottie sat back on his haunches, the picture of dignity again.

Davis watched him in amusement out of the corner of his eye. Scottie was a dog with personality. His brown eyes stared out intelligently from beneath a waterfall effect of hair curving over them. Black hair fell over his mouth to give the effect of sideburns. His little ears were perked up.

Davis placed the chops between slices of toast and began to eat his lunch. Scottie watched him from beneath the waterfall of hair, making no sound, but wrinkling up his nose from time to time. "Well bred, aren't you?" demanded Davis, laughing.

He handed the dog some meat. Scottie took it gravely from his fingers, gave a quick gulp, and the piece of chop was gone. He continued to watch Davis with his intelligent brown eyes. The big powerfully built youth regarded his second sandwich hungrily for a moment, then broke it in two pieces and handed one to the Scotch terrier. "You kind of twist yourself around a chap's heart," said Davis. "If I wasn't leaving all ties behind me, I might adopt you."

The Alabama sun beat down hotly; Scottie wagged his tail approvingly and panted, watching Davis make preparations for departure in his antique car. When the last of the paraphernalia had been packed into the car and water poured on the fire, Scottie climbed up onto the front seat. Davis picked him up and set him down on the ground. "No encumbrances on this trip, old fellow."

Scottie seemed offended at being picked up. He crawled under the car. "Come out from under there!" said Davis, irritation creeping into his voice.

Scottie stared up from beneath his waterfall of hair, but refused to budge. Davis reached under the car and pulled him out. The big fellow shut the door, cranked the car, and climbed in. Scottie stared at him with aggrieved eyes. Then he trotted in front of the car, sat back on his haunches, and panted.

Davis jumped out of the vibrating automobile and picked up a rock. Scottie stared up at him, unmoving. The rock fell from Davis's fingers. "Come on," said the young man gruffly, opening the door, "You can go on with me to Meridian, Mississippi, and there I leave you."

His mother had died a month previous, and Davis had given up his position as accountant in his uncle's firm at Kingston, New York. His uncle had protested, telling him that he would fall heir to the business when he died. Davis, however, did not want to be tied down. He wanted utter freedom.

There had been a girl, too, Sylvia Harrison. Davis had been growing fond of her and had felt it a weakness in himself. A lovely girl was Sylvia, with brown hair lying about her head in soft curls, a straight nose, laughing brown eyes, a quick, intelligent mind. Davis, however, did not want a wife, family, responsibility.

Rain commenced to fall in torrents. The old car jerked and pitched in the rutted road. Scottie stared philosophically ahead through the blurred glass, getting drenched from rain coming in on his side. He sat closer to Davis, seeking warmth. Davis felt grateful for the companionship.

He had been working his way, stopping several weeks in New York, Philadelphia, Washington, and Baltimore, seeing the country as he traveled. He knew he was an excellent accountant, and luck had so far been with him when seeking work.

Davis reached the Mississippi town of Meridian in a cloud burst and registered at a tourist camp. It was a nice town, surprisingly clean and modern. He decided to stay on for a while, but he found no work available. His funds running low, he decided to push on to a larger city while he still had enough to travel on. "Here's where you stay," Davis told Scottie.

Scottie looked up at him with intelligent eyes, wagging his sagebrush tail. Davis walked into a drug store, bought a sandwich, and walked out again, closing the door before the Scotch terrier could follow him outside.

He had walked half a block in the rain, which was still falling fast, when he heard the little black dog scampering after him. Someone had entered the drug store, and Scottie had run out as the door opened. Davis spoke harshly to the little dog, ordering him to go back. Scottie gazed at him with disconsolate eyes, but he did not move. Davis turned his back; the black dog followed. The young man climbed into his car without looking back. Scottie sat back on his haunches, his hair hanging wetly over his unhappy brown eyes; then he leaped on the running board and climbed up between the hood and the fender.

"He can stay there," declared Davis grimly. "I've bothered enough with him."

They were soon outside the town, plunging over the muddy roads. Mud poured back on the little black dog. Finally Davis could stand it no longer. He stopped the car, picked up the little dog roughly, and placed him on the seat. "I'm going to lose you the first chance I get, anyway," he grumbled.

The dog's nose was feverish that night, and Scottie refused food. A pang of repentance stung Davis's heart.

It continued to rain all the way to Hattiesburg. Some days Davis was able to make only fifty miles, and he was worried about Scottie. The little dog still refused to eat. Davis considered his small funds, and stayed at a tourist camp in Hattiesburg. Scottie seemed better the next day, and they started out in high spirits. The skies then opened up.

So it rained all the way across the long Lake Pontchartrain bridge and to New Orleans. Scottie again refused food that night.

Davis sought work, but the Depression had hit this city, too. He wasted shoe leather seeking a position with some of the firms along Canal Street, the main street of the town.

Finally persistence won out. He got two days' work auditing a set of books and received twenty-five dollars in payment. "It will keep me until I can find something regular."

Davis made a discovery, however. The afternoon sun poured into the room he occupied on East Canal Street. Scottie always lay in the middle of the floor, panting, when he reached the boarding house. Davis feared distemper. If he stayed on to find work, his fears might see realization; yet he had scarcely enough money to make the next jump to Houston.

Nevertheless he drove out of New Orleans the next morning through dusty country, to Houston. In that prosperous-looking city, Davis still found nothing to do. "All your fault!" said Davis irritably to the dog. "I should have stayed in New Orleans if it hadn't been for you."

That night he camped on the parched, open prairie. The only landmark within miles was a small trickling stream near the camp. When he returned with an armload of wood, he found Scottie barking excitedly. He had found a rattlesnake behind the tent. Davis killed it and hurled the repulsive reptile away, feeling grateful to the little beast for warning him of the danger.

Scottie sat watching him with dignified interest as he cooked dinner, then he curled up at the foot of Davis's sleeping bag. The young man was awakened out of a sound slumber by a series of excited barks. He leaped up and a black something streaked past him to hurl itself at a hideous coil. The coil straightened, and Scottie ran out of the tent whimpering.

"Snake came back to find its mate!" muttered Davis, the color flowing out of his face.

He heard a faint whimpering sound down by the muddy stream. After killing the rattler with a stick, Davis hurried down to the stream. Scottie had burrowed himself into the mud so that only his nose and eyes were exposed. A dread settled heavily over Davis's heart.

Through the heat of the next day, the little dog stayed buried in the mud. Davis erected a flap over him to protect him from the sun. The young man remembered hearing that dogs could sometimes recover from a rattlesnake's bite by burying themselves immediately in wet mud. He had also heard that milk was supposed to help them dispel the poison. He gave Scottie a pan of it.

The third day Davis found the little terrier at his feet when he awoke, his tail wagging feebly at his adopted master. "You little black sunbeam!" said Davis.

Scottie had entirely recovered when they reached San Antonio. Davis tried to leave him at home while he looked for a job, but Scottie barked so vigorously that he did not dare to. They walked the streets together.

One day Davis halted before a restaurant, tentatively fingering his last fifteen cents, considering whether he should spend it now or the next day. Something was clawing him inside, he was so hungry. Scottie was standing looking up at him through the waterfall of hair, his tongue lolling with heat, fatigue, and hunger, his sagebrush at half-mast. Suddenly he espied a garbage can, walked dispiritedly toward it, and began to chew scraps about it.

Davis's heart constricted. *Is that the way I treat the little fellow who saved my life?* the young man asked himself savagely. He went into a butcher shop and bought fifteen cents worth of hamburger. He then walked to the park and fed it to Scottie.

That afternoon the youth sold his car and other paraphernalia for seventy-five dollars. Before the money was gone, he had a job. He liked his new employer, Mr. Hutchinson, a gray-haired man with a refined manner. The job meant nothing to him, however, except food for himself and Scottie, and a chance to earn enough money for them both to push on to California.

The little dog, shut up all day, did not do well. In three months, he lost his appetite.

Davis diagnosed the matter. "This boarding house isn't the place for him. He needs a place to run, but I can't afford it on what I'm making now." Once more Davis regretted that he had anything to tie him down, but his feeling was not so strong on the subject as it once had been. He began to dream of a little cottage where Scottie could regain his health.

At last Davis found a place with a nice yard. He could not afford the cottage, however, and still save money to continue on to California.

Still the idea burned in his mind, and another idea came with it: *Things would not be so strained if he just earned more money.* He began to take an interest in his work for the first time, working long hours and accomplishing twice the amount he had when he first began working for

Mr. Hutchinson. After two more months, his employer raised his wages, enabling Davis to take the little cottage.

Scottie became a new dog, frisking about him like a puppy. Davis was happier than he had been at any time since he had left Kingston. *Was it possible that one could find happiness in duty well performed?* Davis pondered the thought as he sat evenings on his porch. Then one night he wrote Sylvia Harrison. He was surprised at the quickening of his own heartbeat as he tore open her answering letter with shaking hands. He was hungry to hear from her—and had not known it. Letters were soon flowing back and forth.

One day, a year after his arrival in San Antonio, Davis was called into Mr. Hutchinson's office. "Andrews," said Hutchinson with one of his rare smiles, "I've asked you in here to make you a proposition. I'm getting along in years, and I need a junior partner. Of all the men in my office, you take hold of things the hardest. You don't seem to mind responsibility. I'll arrange to have one-third of my shares transferred to your name before I leave."

Davis stood in frozen silence, something choking up inside him. "I . . . I'd like that, Mr. Hutchinson. Could you give me a month's vacation first to go north? You see," Davis colored slightly, "there's a girl I'd like to marry."

"Fine!" said Mr. Hutchinson heartily. "Then I know you'll be a real success. Nothing develops one like responsibility, Andrews. When you first came here, I sized you up as just another of those 'good-enough' fellows, but without any sense of real responsibility. Then you seemed to change—quite suddenly. This girl, I suppose."

"Later, yes," admitted Davis, grinning. "But it began with wanting to have a better home for a little black dog that once saved my life, Mr. Hutchinson. Then responsibility began to bear its own fruit."

* * * * *

"Scottie Scores a Triumph," by John Scott Douglas. Published January 16, 1932, in *Young People's Weekly*. Reprinted by permission of Joe Wheeler (P. O. Box 12146, Conifer, Colorado 80433) and Cook Communications Ministries, Colorado Springs, Colorado. John Scott Douglas was one of the most prolific and popular writers whose works were published in the leading inspirational and popular magazines during the first half of the twentieth century.

It Isn't Done

M. F. Simmonds

Tom Charters thought he knew what a real gentleman was—until a tree fell on him. It turned out that the epiphany came in the form of a dog—old Don.

* * * * *

On the fragrant pine needles, Vergne Halstead lay at full length, resting his slender strength in utter relaxation. The sleeves of his khaki shirt were rolled to the elbows; a faint breeze stirred the brown hair above his dark eyes. Four others of the camping bunch were there—Art Daley, whittling little old men out of nutshells; Bob Marshall, fiddling with a portable radio; "Shorty" MacLaren, his blue eyes laughing as usual; and Joe Thomas, pale-faced, serene, and happy in a hammock between two pines. Joe would never walk again, but in the old days he had gone to school with Vergne and the crowd, and Vergne had overruled every possible objection to his going on this trip.

"Kitty, kitty, kitty," said Shorty.

Art Daley looked scornfully at the laughing blue eyes, then at the still form of a great collie, lying across the tent floor. The dog's soft brown body was quiet on the ground. His eyes were shut.

"Don's a thoroughbred. You can't get him started that way."

Vergne's dark eyes deepened in affection. "Don's not as young as he used to be. He sleeps more. But there's a lot of life there." The dog, sleeping, had lifted an ear at the tones of his master's voice.

"He sure knows when you speak," Art said, seriously. "He's a gentleman, Don is."

"That's the word," Joe agreed eagerly. "He knows all a gentleman's code. He could play circles around some men I know."

Just then, in the tent door appeared the sixth member of the camping party. Tom Charters wore shiny high-topped boots, new khaki trousers, and a gray-blue flannel shirt cut in the latest mode. Out here in the pine woods of Wisconsin his hair was "slicked" as carefully as if he were ready to attend a reception. Tom Charters was on his way to hunt wintergreen leaves. But old Don lay across the door of the tent.

"Get up!"

Don's eyes opened wide, his ears cocked, but he did not move. He was a gentleman and would not stoop to notice the insult in the tones of command. Vergne's face colored; he opened his lips, but almost before Don could have risen, Tom drew back a shiny-toed boot and kicked.

Then, all at once, things happened. Art Daley dropped nuts and knife and sprang to his feet; the radio was deserted. Shorty ceased to laugh. Joe Thomas moved helplessly in the hammock. Old Don had whirled soundlessly, with open jaws, and Vergne had spoken sharply. "Don! Don! Here, lad! Here, I say!" And the dog came to him.

Vergne stood, one hand clutching the thick brown fur, his chest heaving.

"You talk of being a gentleman, Tom Charters! You have much to learn!"

On Tom's well-trained face appeared a smile that was almost a sneer. "What has being a gentleman to do with making a dog get out of one's way? If the dog doesn't obey, why shouldn't I kick him?"

"Because . . . Don is . . . Don is the real stuff, and it isn't done, Tom. He'd have moved if you'd asked him right."

"I told him to get up. He should have been taught to obey."

"He obeys a gentleman." Vergne's eyes were flashing. Tom's face flushed an instant, then he laughed.

"So? Then he'll learn to obey me." And he walked off down the slope beneath the whispering pines.

"Whew! I thought you were going to knock him down, Vergne." Art Daley dropped limply at the foot of the big pine.

"Why didn't you? He needed it! Don is a gentleman, and any fool ought to know better than to speak to him like that. Don knows Tom anyhow. Don't you notice how he bristles whenever he comes near?"

Shorty MacLaren's hands were trembling. Vergne's fingers shook a little, too.

"I . . . I did want to knock him down," he confessed. "But I couldn't, of course. It isn't done."

Down on the ground he went, by the dog. Bob Marshall came over by him, his radio forgotten.

"Why do you always say that, Vergne? Oh, not always, but I've heard you say it a lot."

Vergne looked uneasy. "I hardly know how to explain it. But with all his airs, Tom isn't a real gentleman. I can't put it into words, but there are a few things in life that just are not done by a real man. The man who does those things is no gentleman."

"You're right, Vergne," Joe spoke feelingly. "For all his sophistication and fine manners, Tom doesn't know what a gentleman is. You fellows wanted me. I know I'm a drag on the fun, but I know you like the drag. But Tom says and looks things . . . well, he never lets a fellow forget."

The eyes of the four were all on Joe Thomas. Shorty MacLaren's took on a suspicious moisture, and his face worked.

"Now I *will* knock him down . . . and wipe up the earth with him!"

"No, you won't, Shorty. Vergne is right—it isn't done. That wouldn't teach him a thing. I don't mind . . . much. I'm too glad to be here with the rest of you to let him spoil it."

"What's he here for anyhow?" Art Daley burst out. "Why did we bring him?"

Bob Marshall at last answered. "I hardly know, unless because he was new in town, and there were just five of the old crowd left, and we thought six would be more fun."

"He always talked about camping and seemed a regular fellow," Shorty contributed.

"And he has manners, you'll have to admit that." Joe smiled as he said it. "He has all the earmarks of a gentleman."

"Isn't it funny," mused Shorty, "how the little things show up a fellow? We've seen a lot of him, and he's usually mannerly and courteous. But things like kicking Don—and making Joe feel that way . . ."

"And those little things, sooner or later, come to be big ones," said Art. "He's got to learn."

Vergne Halstead gave old Don a final hug.

"Well, fellows, I guess we can't teach him. I don't see a thing to do but just go on acting square ourselves. Maybe something will happen."

"It would take a real miracle to teach Tom Charters, though," Art said assuredly and viciously attacked another nutshell. Bob went back to the radio, Shorty to his dreaming, Joe to his book. And Vergne rose and walked away with old Don. He needed time to think. Old Don had belonged to him since he was a fat little puppy. The dog was a gentleman, with a gentleman's code. Vergne would rather have been struck himself than to have seen Tom kick the loyal old collie. It took a long tramp to bring him back to the tent with a calm face, ready to laugh at Tom's wit.

That was one of the things that made it hard. Tom was cheerful, witty; he had traveled much and could talk entertainingly; he kept up his share of the work. But there was something lacking. The boys no longer felt at ease in his presence, for it seemed, as they knew him better, that he constantly held himself above them, that he knew too well that he was entertaining. But there was nothing to be done about it.

A day later, Vergne came up to the tent at dusk from a swim in the little river. Long blue shadows had settled under the pines. The sky was crowded with a great piled storm which had come suddenly, as Wisconsin storms do. It was a full two hours before dusk should have crept into the tent. Vergne had shortened his time in the water and come home alongside a dripping brown dog.

Joe was inside the tent on his cot. The hammock was down, and the boys were fastening tent pegs more securely, endeavoring to make themselves as safe as possible.

"Where's Tom?"

"He strolled off about two—don't you remember?"

"Hasn't he come back yet?" Vergne was alert.

"No—he'll be along."

Vergne stood a minute, uncertain. He went into the tent and busied himself at his suitcase.

"I'll just go over to the Chimney Rock and give him a call or two. He's asleep somewhere, perhaps, and he's due for a good wetting if he is."

"Well, better hurry. The storm'll be here soon."

Vergne laughed. "You know me in storms. I'll take care of myself."

And he was off, with old Don keeping pace. As soon as he had gone beyond their sight, Vergne quickened his steps. The old crowd had camped here before and knew every foot of the way. But it was Tom Charters's first trip, and he had been restless to explore Rattlesnake Bluff ever since his arrival. The boys had postponed going with him.

But Vergne was sure that Tom had gone alone, now, to the bluff. Once started on its winding rocky ledges beneath the pines, it was easy to lose the one safe path downward. A storm on Rattlesnake Bluff was a terrible thing. The boys had once been there at such a time and had crouched with blanched faces in a hollow of rock and earth while destruction raged around them. Tom was not used to Wisconsin.

Vergne broke into an easy run, meanwhile wrapping his safety matchbox in a handkerchief and putting it deep in a pocket, and putting another handkerchief around his revolver. *Had Tom taken his?* he wondered. There were occasionally strange reports about sights and sounds on the grim old bluff, so the wise ones went armed.

The bluff, towering high with sheer rock walls, stretched for a mile over the countryside. By the time Vergne had run the first mile, quick as he was, the wind was beginning to bend the slough grass flat. By the time the second mile was ended, big drops started to come. Vergne increased his speed, but it was a wet boy and a wet dog who crept into the shelter of a low cavelike hollow at the base of the bluff. It was a real Wisconsin cloudburst.

The lightning made the sky an almost continuous sheet of flame; the thunder was deafening. Vergne assured himself that his matches and revolver were dry, then gathered old Don close, for the dog had shaken himself and was already drying. In silence, they watched the downpour of rain, driven in wild sheets by the terrific wind. The storm increased in fury each minute, and presently a great tree crashed down from the top of the bluff. Don moved uneasily and glanced at his master with a question in his eyes.

"It's all right, old boy," Vergne reassured him. But his thoughts were on Tom Charters.

When the worst of the storm had passed on, Vergne spoke again. "Well, Don, how about trying it?"

Don wagged his tail and looked his consent. He did not understand their mission, but he would go anywhere with his master. Vergne put safety matches and revolver inside the front of his shirt where the wide belt crossed it and they would be protected from the rain. He had not gone ten feet up the path before his shoulders and back were dripping, for the rain was still constant.

At the top, he and Don wandered about uncertainly. Vergne's first thought was to fire a shot and see if he could get an answer. But the rain and the wind in the pine trees seemed to him to make noise enough to drown the sound. After stumbling about for fifteen minutes, he decided to wait a bit for the storm to lessen. He flashed his light. He was near the great old pine whose trunk would form some shelter for him and the dog. Into the darkness he plunged again. Old Don seemed to grasp the idea and with a short bark leaped forward, his eyes glowing in the darkness. Vergne followed hastily. And then a shot rang out, followed by a series of agonized barks. A dog in pain utters such sounds of agony as cut to the heart. Vergne's light went on; he fumbled for his revolver, as he sprang forward, shouting, "Tom! Is that you, Tom? It's Vergne and Don—don't shoot! Don't shoot!"

Old Don half lay, half sat on the ground, now, trying to lick a place where the white fur was becoming red. Vergne fairly flung himself at him, all else forgotten. A quick examination convinced him that the dog was not seriously hurt, the bullet having gone through the fleshy part of his neck. Then a sound of sobbing penetrated to his frantic mind.

He swept the flashlight quickly over the ground ahead. The great pine was down! And the sobbing came from it. Soon Vergne was tugging at the immense trunk. The pine had crashed down across a little depression, and in that depression lay Tom Charters on his side, pinned down, drenched, sobbing, a revolver in his hand.

"Tom! Tom! It's Vergne!" and his strong hands shook the boy's shoulders. "Everything's all right; it was just Don you saw. Can't you move?"

Tom's head moved negatively. Vergne tried again to lift the trunk, but in a few minutes convinced himself that it was impossible. Moreover, the air was cool now. Tom would at least be stiff and sore, and Don had a bullet hole through his neck. He could not take them both down. He brought the dog over to Tom.

"Lie down—closer—lie down, Don." The dog moved nearer to Tom and lay down beside him. Vergne took out a handkerchief and laid it against the white throat.

"Can you keep that there, Tom? It may help some. Do you have a flashlight?"

"No . . . no."

Vergne was genuinely sorry. "I can't leave mine or I'll waste time getting down, and I dare not leave the matchbox, for these pine needles burn like tinder; they'd burn in an ocean, almost. But Don will guard you, and I'll bring the boys at once. Cheer up, Tom. You're safe enough. Don't shoot the next time. We'll call as we come."

Vergne laid a big tender hand on the dog's head. "Guard him, old boy! I'll come back."

Then he was gone, and with him went the world for old Don, and all thoughts of safety for Tom. But when Tom started breathing heavily and chokily again, old Don whined uneasily and moved closer. Presently he was lying tightly pressed against the boy, and when another long breath came, he touched Tom Charters's cheek with a cold, worried nose.

When Vergne came back with the boys, with axes and lights and blankets and the means to improvise a stretcher, he found Tom's hand still holding the now-red handkerchief to the dog's throat and his other arm wound tightly about the brown shoulders. Tom had little to say while the boys put a blanket about his shivering back and began to tug at the old pine. The storm had nearly died. He did not find words even when they extricated him and he'd been carried back to camp and made warm and dry. He was so lame all over from lying in the cramped position, that every movement was agony. But he was sure he was not really hurt.

It was the next afternoon, as he lay on his cot, that Vergne happened to be alone with him, dressing old Don's wound. Tom watched him.

"Vergne," he said at last, "I've made a big mistake. I thought a great deal while I waited for you to bring help. I've always wanted to be a gentleman—a real one. I thought it was what you said and did that made you one. But it isn't. It's what you *are*. And yet I don't quite see some things about it—how you get to be what no one can really tell you about!"

Vergne smiled, his dark eyes friendly. "It's a funny sort of thing, I know. You can't tell what it is, but some day, you just understand. You just know." He patted the dog's head. Tom went on.

"There's another thing, Vergne. I can't for the life of me figure out why Don stayed, why he got closer to me and tried to keep me warm and comfort me. I know you didn't want him hurrying back through the rain with the bullet hole in his neck, but why didn't he try to go? Why didn't he growl at me? I've kicked him. I had just shot him. Why didn't he get even? Or at least try to go away?"

Verne's eyes were shining. "It isn't done," he said quietly. "Don is a gentleman."

And into the eyes of Tom Charters came a new look. He understood.

* * * * *

"It Isn't Done," by M. F. Simmonds. Published March 8, 1927, in *The Youth's Instructor*. Reprinted by permission of Joe Wheeler (P. O. Box 1246, Conifer, Colorado 80433) and Review and Herald Publishing Association, Hagerstown, Maryland. M. F. Simmonds wrote for turn-of-the-twentieth-century inspirational and popular magazines.

When Tad Remembered

Minnie Leona Upton

Mary Merivale turned and peered eagerly down the length of the quiet elm-shaded street; then, the expectant light faded from her tired eyes. She had done this a full five thousand times—but still no Bobbie.

That was bad enough, but where was Taddy—Taddy, her beloved dog?

This story dates back about a hundred years ago, to a time when diseases such as diphtheria, typhoid, scarlet fever, cholera, tuberculosis, and influenza, when they came, wiped out entire families—there being no known antidotes. When you add in death because of childbirth complications, you were lucky if half your children survived to adulthood. It was a mighty tough and heartbreaking time in which to live.

This is an old story, and I have loved it ever since I first heard it, growing up. I have never been able to find anything about the author. In fact, this is the only one of her stories I have ever found. What a pity!

* * * * *

It was closing time for a little notion shop that shyly besought the scant patronage of a sleepy, shabby old side street in a great city. The little notion-shop lady sped a last lingering patron with a cheery, but decided, good-night, then following her outside, closed the snow-burdened blinds with tremulous haste, and, turning, peered eagerly down the length of the quiet, elm-lined street. One long look, then the patient eyes from which the expectant light had suddenly faded, turned for a moment to the remote, keen December stars, and a tired little sigh accompanied the clicking of the key in the lock.

Full five thousand times had Mary Merivale done this, and nothing more interesting than Sandy MacPherson, the cobbler, putting up his shutters or old Bettina, the apple woman, ambling homeward with empty basket had yet rewarded her searching gaze. But it was part of her day, of her life, and the warm thrill of unreasoning hope had never failed to come. Next time—who could tell? Especially at Christmas time!

She hung the key on its nail and limped back into her low-ceiled sitting-room/dining-room/kitchen. With resolute cheerfulness she opened the drafts and woke the slumbering fire in the shining stove, lit the rose-shaded lamp, drew the curtains, and filled the diminutive teakettle. She was beginning to spread a white cloth on the wee round table (having removed the Dresden shepherdess and the pot of pansies and the crocheted doily and the cretonne cover), when her operations were interrupted by a vigorous scratching on the door opening into the backyard.

The little lady's face broke into a welcoming smile, deepening a host of pleasant wrinkles. She drew the bolt; the door burst open; and in bounded a little rough-coated, brownish-yellow—or yellowish-brown—mongrel, yapping joyously and springing up, albeit somewhat laboriously and rheumatically, to bestow exuberant kisses upon the beloved hands of his lady.

"There, there, Taddy. There, there, that'll do," she said.

But there was not a marked firmness in the prohibition, and it was several minutes before Tad subsided and sank, with asthmatic wheezes, upon a braided rug that looked as if it might have been made from Joseph's "coat of many colors."

"Been watchin' for the rat, Taddy?"

Tad thumped the mat with his happy, lowbred, undocked tail. He took no shame to himself that a year's efforts had failed to catch and bring to justice the canny old rat that, under the waste-barrel house, made carefree entrances and exits through a hole that led to regions unknown. He knew nothing of the countless times when the bold bandit had skipped nonchalantly forth while he was taking forty winks.

Once the villain would not have escaped him so arrogantly, nor, indeed, at all! But almost twenty conscientiously active years, with asthma and rheumatism, had stolen away, bit by bit, his alertness of observation and elasticity of muscle, though not one iota of his warmth of heart and lightness of spirit.

He curled up contentedly on his rug and watched proceedings with eager interest, now and then putting out an affectionately arresting paw when his mistress whisked near him in her bustling to and fro.

Presently his bowl of broth was set down before him, on a square of blue-and-white oilcloth, and his lady sat herself down to her own frugal meal. It ended with a tiny square of fruitcake (brought in by an old customer) for the lady—and a lump of moist brown sugar for the dog.

"If you'd only chew it, Tad, 'pears to me you'd taste it more," observed Tad's mistress, in a tone of gentle reproach.

Tad promptly assumed an expression of penitence and hopefulness, fetchingly blended—penitence, not from any reason of the nature of his offense, but because that tone in her voice always indicated that he had done something, and hopefulness, because of the expectation of a small supplementary lump which he had hitherto received. He saw no reason this night why the second lump should not continue. But tonight—tonight—no second lump was forthcoming.

The little woman spoke apologetically, "Tomorrow, I hope, Taddy dear, perhaps three lumps. Who knows? Business hasn't been very good this week [she had sold just seven cents' worth of 'notions,' and the rent was due], and I never ask for it, you know."

Tad didn't know. But he felt the sorrow in the dear voice. He got up, stiffly, and laid his common little head in her lap, and looked comforting volumes with his great shining eyes. He licked the queer salty water that dropped on her hand from somewhere, and she began to smile and call him her "comfort," whereat he wagged hilariously.

Presently Mrs. Maguire, who had moved in next door, and whose red, white, and blue sign read, "Washing And Scrubbing Dun Inside or Out," ran in for a friendly chat. Neighborliness burgeons at Christmas time!

"A foine loively little dawg, Mis' Merivale!" she commented enthusiastically, directing an approving pat at Tad's rough head. It descended on air. Tad had flopped over on one side and was lying with one paw raised appealingly, one eye alertly open, and the other tightly closed.

"Was ivver the loikes av thot, now, for the way of a dawg!" exclaimed the admiring Mrs. Maguire.

But Mary Merivale had dropped on her knees beside the little performer, tears and smiles playing hide-and-seek among her wrinkles.

"It's a trick my Bobbie taught 'im, when he was yet a wee-bit puppy near twenty years ago. Who's Bobbie? Why . . . but there, you're a newcomer in the neighborhood. Bobbie is my little boy. That is, he *was* my little boy. I . . . Mis' Maguire, there's something about you makes me feel you'd understand; somehow my heart and my head have been full of remembering today. I . . . I would so like to tell you about Bobbie and how it is that I'm alone—if it wouldn't tire you after your hard day's work."

"Mis' Merivale, just lit it pourr right out! It'll do the hearts of the two ov us good—you to pourr it out, an' me to take it in! I brought me Moike's sweater to darrn, an' its a good listenin' job."

A big red hand gave the soft gray waves of Mary Merivale's hair a gentle pat; then Mrs. Maguire began to rock to and fro, as she threaded a huge darning needle and essayed to fill in a ragged aperture.

Mary Merivale, knitting swiftly on a sturdy red mitten, took up her story.

"Nineteen years ago last October, my husband died—the kindest, best husband that ever lived. But we'd never been able to save much, havin' had eight children in the seventeen years we'd been married, and all of them went with diphtheria except Bobbie. So doctor's bills and funeral expenses kept us in debt, the best we could do.

"And somehow, when John left me, I went all in a heap, and I was sick a long time, and when I got around again, I didn't seem to have any strength or courage. So when a nice old couple with money offered to adopt Bobbie and give him the best education money could pay for, I felt that I ought to let him go. I never could have done for him that way.

"He was such a bright little fellow—seven years old, and could read right off in the Bible and the *Old Farmers' Almanac* without stoppin' to spell out hardly a word! Mr. and Mrs. Brown—that was their name—took to him from the start. They had him take their name at the very first. That did hurt somehow, though 'twas right. And kind of them. They'd just bought a fine place over in the next town to Benfield, where I'd always lived, and first I thought I'd see Bobbie often. But they didn't seem to like very well to see me come. What? Oh, no . . . no! They were very kind, but I guess they thought it kept Bobbie too much stirred up to have Taddy and me droppin' in every little once in a while. I'd a left Taddy with him, but Mrs. Brown didn't like dogs.

"Well, that winter they sold their new place and went away, and they fixed it so I never could find out their address . . ."

"The sthony-hearrted crathurs!" exploded Mrs. Maguire, sitting bolt upright and dropping Mike's sweater. "Hiv'n'll punish . . . "

"Oh, no, no, Mrs. Maguire, they thought they were doing the best for Bobbie. They wanted to make a gentleman of him . . . and so did I. And finally I saw 'twas selfish of me to try to keep a hold on him, when he had such a good chance to grow up different, somehow; and I stopped tryin' to trace him up.

"Well, instead of gainin' strength, I seemed to lose it, after I got to work a while. I tried to give up the washin' and scrubbin' that I'd tried to do. So when I heard from my husband's cousin Mary—she used to dressmake on this street, but she went back to Benfield for her last sickness—that this little shop was for sale, with the good will and fixtures and stock, I took the bit of money that was left after the house was sold and the debts paid, and came here to the city and started for myself.

"Hard? Yes, it seemed so, for John had always stood between me and business. Still, I'm not the only one that's had to bear hard things. And I've made a livin'.

"But even so, if it hadn't been for Taddy, I don't know what I'd have done! He was a puppy then, and just as bright for a dog as Bobbie was for a

←————————————————————————————————→

boy. Bobbie taught him a lot of the regular tricks such as other dogs do, but this one he just did was one that Bobbie himself invented. It was intended for an apology, and Taddy was to do it whenever he thought he'd been naughty.

"Well, at first after Bobbie went, Taddy'd never do it except when I took him to see Bobbie. But after Bobbie went where we couldn't visit him any more, the little fellow began to do it for me, whenever he saw me lookin' downhearted. The little scalawag had noticed that it made folks laugh, and so he thought 'twould answer that purpose, as well as be an apology. At least, I'm pretty sure that was what was in Taddy's mind.

"But now, for a long time, he hasn't done it. Got out of the way of it when his rheumatism was bad. But this evenin' he saw I was a bit down—this raw weather is so tryin', don't you think?—and that reminded him, bless his heart!

"Haven't I ever heard anything of Bobbie? I was comin' to that. Two years ago, an old Benfield neighbor who was sightseein' here in the city thought she saw Bobbie with a lot of medical students goin' into one of the new buildin's of the medical school. She said he looked just as she *knew* Bobbie'd look, grown up. And I thought maybe 'twas here the Browns lived—Benfield's only twenty-five miles out—and it seemed real likely, somehow, that Bobbie'd be learnin' to be a doctor, for he was always doctorin' up sick dogs and cats and birds. I went right out to the school, leavin' Miss Jenks, the neighbor, to tend shop. Seemed as though I couldn't get there soon enough. But no, there wasn't any Robert Brown there studyin'. All the strength went out of me. Not that I meant to thrust myself on him and mortify him, when he'd got to be a gentleman, but I just thought I could plan to see him, once in a while, as he went in and out."

Mrs. Maguire made a noncommittal sound, something between a sob and a grunt. Mary Merivale went on, unheeding.

"No, I'd never thrust myself on him. But somehow, I know it's weak and selfish, but somehow, way down in my heart, I've never give up the idea that sometime Bobbie'd trace *me* out. Mis' Maguire, I've never said this to another livin' bein'. But some way, 'twould seem like Bobbie . . .

"He's twenty-six now, almost. When I go out to close the shop blind at night I can almost *see* him comin' along the street, with his fine, big square shoulders back, and his head up! He looked so much like his father when he was little that I'm almost sure he looks *just* like him now.

"Yes, yes, Mis' Maguire, it is a true sayin'—'If it wa'n't for hope, the heart would break!' Yes, thank God for hope!

"Must you go now? Well, it *is* gettin' late—I've run on so. Yes, I *will* run in soon. Real neighborin' *is* such a comfort. And I can talk freer to you than I ever could to anybody else. You don't try to . . . plan for me or criticize. Just sit and listen, with your face so kind. Rather go in at your back door? Then I'll go out with you to the back gate for a bit o' fresh air."

Tad politely preceded the two, as escort. But just outside the gate he caught sight of his ancient foe, the cobbler's big gray cat, and started in ardent pursuit.

"He'll soon be back!" laughed his mistress and propped the gate ajar with a brick and left the back door open a bit, as she went about her preparations for the night.

But Tad did not come back, triumphant over a routed foe or comically disgruntled over one who had proved far too quick for him.

All night his mistress lay broad awake, getting up every few minutes to go out in the alley and call and listen—but in vain! Morning came at last, and she rose listlessly and opened the little shop, prepared her scanty breakfast and cleared it away—untouched.

She laid the case before her paper boy, and he enthusiastically enlisted all the neighborhood boys in the search. Heart and soul, and alert eyes and nimble legs, they entered into it, for they were all loyal to Tad and his mistress, and not a boy but was glad to do the little notion-shop lady a good turn. Such multitudinously active good will was an unspeakable comfort—but it did not result in Tad.

The first day dragged interminably away, then another, and another. Mary Merivale went out early on that third day to close her blinds. She could not bear to see another customer.

Almost she did not look up and down the street.

"What's the use?" sighed a gray little whisper. But then her brave heart

←——————————————————————————————→

lifted itself once more. She stepped far out on the sidewalk and raised her eyes.

Around the corner of the street, bright under the last level sunshine of a perfect December day, a little shape trotted happily in front of a stalwart figure—tall, white-clad. Then a succession, no, a tangle, of joyous yaps sounded on the still air.

Mary Merivale ran forward a few unsteady steps and stopped. The athletic figure, seen in the radiant sunlight, through her tears, looked like a tall, haloed angel. Strong arms closed around her, and warm kisses rained on her forehead, her lips, her cheeks, her hair!

"Motherdee!"

"Bobbie!"

Suddenly Tad stopped jumping up and trying to climb to their shoulders. They looked down, through joyful tears. There he lay, an appealing paw up, one eye alertly open, and the other screwed tight shut!

"Oh, Mother, Mother, 'twas *that* that did it—found you, I mean! Oh, Mother, I tried so hard to trace you, for a while, after I got to be a big fellow, in high school, and . . . and sensed things. But I couldn't, for the people who knew where you'd moved when you gave up the old house had died or gone nobody knew where, and all my letters came back. Finally, I was told you were dead. And the name and the age in the paper were the same."

"That was your father's cousin Mary. But never mind—now!"

"Oh, Mother! And then old Mr. Brown and his wife died suddenly. They'd looked out for me, legally, you know. But the relatives were so . . . so jealous that I vowed I'd never take a cent of the money. And I didn't! I'd got a start, and I've worked my way. And I took back my own name, Mother—*our* name!"

"I'm so proud of you; go on, Bobbie boy!"

"Well, I worked my way through college and medical school, and I'm to graduate this year—from this school right here in the city. Mother, think! Here all these years, three years, and never found each other! How can such things be?

"And today, Mother, oh, Mother, we . . . we . . . Mother, I thought I ought to do it for the good of humanity, but I'll never have part in any such thing again . . . never! I'll learn some other way! Today we were going to experiment on a dog. Yes, a live dog! And everything was ready, and the dog was brought in, and, oh, I'd done such things often enough, and we were joking and laughing. But somehow there was a look in this dog's eyes that . . . that . . . well, all of a sudden I wanted to cry. I felt myself choking up, and I stooped down and patted him, and what did the little chap do but whop over and perform that blessed old trick! Then I remembered; then I *knew!*

"And, Mother, they say medical students get calloused and are a hardhearted lot. But if you could have seen them and the great surgeon who was to conduct the experiment—we'd had it set late, out of regular hours, to get him—if only you could have seen them, you'd have said their hearts were all right, I can tell you!

"They all came out with me, and Tad struck a bee line for home—*home,* Mother! And I couldn't believe I'd find you, but I thought I'd find out *about* you and where to put the beautiful headstone I meant to buy when I got to earning money, which will be as soon as I graduate, Mother, for a fine old doctor with a big practice is going to take me in with him! And I was hurrying along, when I heard a woman sing out, 'An' sure there's Mary Merivale's dawg, praise the saints!' And then I couldn't come fast enough, and Tad couldn't, either! And then, oh Mother, I saw you standing there with the sunshine on your dear hair and your sweet eyes shining—the blessed, beautiful eyes that I remembered so well! And then, oh, Mother!"

"Bobbie!"

There was a silence. Then the deep young voice spoke, reverently, as men speak of holy things. "And it's Christmas Eve, Mother."

The radiant eyes shone up into his.

And Tad? He dutifully began a repetition of his star act, but had his eye only half shut, when he was caught up and carried into the house, his head snuggled down on a broad shoulder, beside a dear, illuminated face, from which he promptly and efficiently licked the queer salty water.

* * * * *

"When Tad Remembered," by Minnie Leona Upton. Published December 22, 1925, in *The Youth's Instructor*. Reprinted by permission of Joe Wheeler (P. O. Box 1246, Conifer, Colorado 80433) and Review and Herald Publishing Association, Hagerstown, Maryland. Minnie Leona Upton wrote for inspirational and popular magazines during the first half of the twentieth century.

Captain Kidd's Ribbons

Dee Dunsing

Milly May was angry. Of all the nerve! That stuck-up Hugh Edgerton whose dog, Captain Kidd, always beat her dogs in shows, asking her to . . .

It was just too much, that's what it was!

* * * * *

Milly May gathered up sponge, towel, brush, soap, and a blanket that she had thoughtfully brought along to keep Rusty Boy warm. She wore a fixed smile. Even if your dog has failed to win a prize for five years in a row, smiling is expected. It is the traditionally sporting thing to do.

Rusty Boy's dark hazel eyes showed his humiliation. Milly May couldn't fool him. He sensed the disappointment beneath her smile. In spite of all the parading around a show ring, in spite of the judge's exceptional interest, he realized that he had failed.

Seeing his hurt, Milly May gave him a consoling pat on one wiry-haired shoulder. "Never mind, Rusty Boy. You'll win a ribbon somewhere, sometime. You're a good dog. It's just that . . . well, I guess no Welch terrier in the United States could beat Captain Kidd."

She glanced across the ring to where Hugh Edgerton was exhibiting his prizewinner. Photographers were taking Captain Kidd's picture for use in newspapers and dog magazines. Hugh looked up and nodded at her. It was the same cold, distant nod, tinged with arrogance and pride, that he had always given.

She turned quickly and led Rusty Boy out of the building toward her coupé. All the while she kept telling herself, as she had for years, that her dogs were good dogs. They were blooded dogs with champion forebears—maybe not so many as Captain Kidd had, but enough to produce prizewinners. And she had raised them so carefully, sparing no bit of trouble or affection to make them the happiest, healthiest dogs in any kennel. They weren't scrubs, she reiterated. They might all have been champions if Hugh Edgerton's father had not bought him Captain Kidd. It was just that the Captain was exceptional even among good dogs.

It rained before she reached home, a steady pelting downpour that flowed across the roads like a river. All that afternoon and evening it rained. Trees drooped and wailed in the wind. The sky was a solid gray. The ground became as soggy as Rusty Boy's sponge.

Milly May trotted back and forth to her kennels with an old slicker over her head. She petted the dogs and talked to them, trying to console them for the dismal weather. They missed sunshine and their customary exercise, which Milly May was afraid to give them because the runways were twisting streams.

When the rain kept on, she moved all the young puppies and two or three of the older dogs into the garage, which had a good floor and was warm. Her coupé had to be left outside in the rain. It was precious, but not as precious as the pups.

As the rain persisted, the river rose swiftly. Already it had spread across its flood plain, inundating fields of corn, which waved beneath the water like moss. A few houses close to the river banks had been swept away, and a great many more were threatened. People living in the danger areas were evacuating.

"Another week of this, and we'll have the worst flood in history," Milly May's father said, shaking his head.

He wasn't frightened for himself or his family. Their home was on a hill, the highest in the city. He was remembering the last flood with its homeless thousands, its starvation and suffering.

The rain continued. The front porches of houses were drowned in the river, and water was seeping in under the doors. A few people who had been slow to move were obliged to use boats for getting in and out of their homes. Stalled automobiles lined the river road. It was a pathetic scene of wrecked human effort and halted activity.

Then miraculously the rain stopped, and the sun came out. Milly May breathed a long sigh of relief. The pups had come through all right, with no distemper and only a cold or two among them. People would be safe again. Soon the water would drain off, and the world would be sunny and bright. She resolved that she would never again complain as long as there was sunshine to enjoy.

That same morning, she received a long-distance call from Wisconsin. It was from Hugh Edgerton. His voice was so excited and shaky that she scarcely recognized it.

"I've been in Wisconsin, out in the country," he explained hastily. "Didn't see a paper until just now, about the floods. Say, Milly May, I've got to ask a favor of you. I'll pay you if you'll do it."

"I don't need pay," replied Milly May impatiently. "What is it you want?"

"It's about Captain Kidd," he went on. "I'm scared that something has happened to him. The caretaker's probably skipped out by now on account of flood danger. Would you—I know it's asking a lot—would you go up and see if the dog's all right?"

"Why, why yes," replied Milly May, too surprised at this request to say more.

"Thanks." Hugh's voice was warm. "I'll entrust the Captain entirely to you."

Milly May hung up the receiver with a dazed look. Hugh Edgerton asking a favor of her, asking her to watch after Captain Kidd—of all dogs! Why, he had been her jinx for five years. He had beaten her out of so many ribbons that it made her dizzy to think about them.

The more she thought about Hugh's request, the angrier she became. It was like kicking somebody till your boot wore out and then asking him to please mend the toe. And she had consented as meekly as a lamb!

She remembered Hugh at the various dog shows. He had never talked to her, hadn't even been friendly. She had put him down as a snob. *But even snobs needed people to run errands for them,* she thought bitterly.

Since she had promised, there was nothing she could do but drive out to Hugh's house and look after the dog. She took the rubber ponchos off the coupé's radiator, found that the little car would run, and started out.

Through rain-drenched streets she wound toward Hugh's home, which stood at one end of the heights above the river. As she stopped before the spacious house, she realized that it was safe from the flood, but that its backyard was probably engulfed.

Still angry with herself for performing this favor, she hopped out of her car and hurried around to the rear entrance. A broad lawn with well-kept shrubs showed the skilled professional hand of a gardener. No wonder Hugh's father had been able to buy Captain Kidd! A man who lived in a place like this could probably buy a whole kennel full of thoroughbreds, the finest in the land. He wouldn't need to conduct his business on a shoestring the way she did.

As she rounded the house, she came upon a startling sight. Three hundred feet away where the lawn sloped sharply toward the river stood Captain Kidd's kennel. Only the peak of its roof was out of water. The entire pen was under water, the high wire fence around it standing only a foot or so above the overflow. On the narrow bit of kennel roof stood Captain Kidd himself, drenched to the skin—shivering and desolate. For days he must have stood there braving exposure, going without food, seeing his little shingle island disappear inch by inch. But pathetic as his condition was, he would not howl or complain. He would only wait, as a champion should do.

Milly May's heart contracted with pity, but she tried to harden it. This was the dog who had stolen all the glory for so long. The dog she had loathed as being too perfect. She would have to get him out to safety. And for what? So that he could go on winning ribbons, shutting her dogs out.

Well, she was here. She had promised Hugh to do this favor, and she would do it. She pursed her lips and gave a long whistle. Captain Kidd looked at her, one of his ears cocked hopefully. But he did not move.

She wondered why he didn't answer her call. Then suddenly she realized that the gate was locked against him. That was the reason he had been forced to stay on top of his kennel. He was a prisoner in his own yard.

She glanced at the water between her and the pen door, trying to estimate its depth. Perhaps she could wade out there—or perhaps she couldn't. It might be too deep, or the sluggish current too strong. But something had to be done. Whether she wished to or not, she must rescue Captain Kidd.

With a decisive motion she sat down on the back stairs and removed her heavy Oxfords. Then she waded out into the water. It was cold, curling over her toes, then her ankles. To her alarm, the wash rapidly got deeper. Its strong, slow current tugged at her. The hem of her skirt got wet, and she hadn't gone half the distance to the gate.

For an instant she paused. There was no other way. She would have to swim it.

With an angry splashing, she waded on. Abruptly the water rose high. She struck out with a strong swimming stroke. If it took every dime she had, she would beat Captain Kidd at the dog show next year. This subjection to indignity would spur her on. She would do it somehow, she vowed to herself.

Swimming was awkward with her clothes hanging on her like heavy weights. The current strove to pull her downstream, clutching at her with icy, imperious fingers. A dead tree branch floated past and scratched her cheek. But, lashed on by her anger, she plowed ahead, digging her arms into the strong-willed water.

From his place on the kennel roof Captain Kidd was watching her. Although he looked incredibly skinny and bedraggled, his erect ears and alert carriage were those of a champion. Once or twice he gave an eager little whine as if he wanted to help.

Then Milly May had reached the fence, was grasping its wire meshes, drawing herself toward the locked gate. The wire cut into her palms, but that didn't matter. She was almost through with this job.

She reached the gate, lifted its hook. The current was with her now, flinging the gate wide. Milly May pursed her lips and let out a long whistle.

But Captain Kidd hadn't waited to be summoned. With a hoarse bark he had leaped into the swollen river and was swimming toward her.

Milly May started swimming back, and the two of them emerged safe and secure at almost the same minute. While Milly May wrung water out of her clothes, Captain Kidd shook himself violently from the tip of his muzzle to the end of his stubby tail as if to say, "Well, I certainly am glad to be through with that experience!"

It was only while Milly May was pulling on her Oxfords that she realized something unusual had happened. Captain Kidd came and stood close to her. Abruptly he reached out and licked her wet hands. Then he looked up at her with something in his eyes that startled Milly May.

"Well, I'll be jiggered," she remarked in amazement.

For there was no mistaking that caress and that look. Captain Kidd knew what she had done, and he was grateful. More than that: he loved her. Plainly that light in his eyes was worship.

Milly May felt a strange sensation around her own heart. It wasn't anger or resentment after all. It was—well, yes, it was love, too. She had always known that Captain Kidd deserved those ribbons. He was a real champion. More than color, or pointed ears, or formation of skull and nose, this incident proved it to her.

She patted his coarse, wet-haired back with a mixture of tenderness and roughness. "I'll take back everything I ever thought about you, Captain," she said.

* * *

Hugh was home in two days. When he called at Milly May's house for his dog, he still seemed distant and aloof.

"Thanks for taking care of the Captain," he said as he took the dog's leash. "When I got your letter, telling what had happened, I thought . . . well, I thought . . ."

He paused, and for the first time Milly May saw that Hugh's aloofness was not caused by pride but by a terrible shyness. She was too amazed to speak.

"I thought," Hugh struggled on, "that it would have been mighty . . . well, mighty awful, if anything had happened."

Milly May smiled warmly. She might be poor, but she wasn't shy. And there was lots of talking to do to make up for those five aloof years. How stupid she had been to think Hugh was a snob just because he had money and a champion dog.

"I was glad to help," she told him. "I'll always be glad any time you ask me."

Hugh smiled less awkwardly. "You've been awfully sporting," he observed, "considering that . . . well, considering that Captain took so many ribbons away from you. I didn't mean, when I showed him the first time, that he should monopolize everything. But he . . . well, he's just that kind of dog. He can't help it. And it didn't seem fair to keep him out."

Milly May nodded. "The best dog wins." She smiled above a lump in her throat, a lump that didn't have anything to do with prizes at dog shows but was solely because in a minute or so she would have to part with Captain Kidd. Somehow in these two days she had almost felt that he was her own dog, as much as Rusty Boy and all the others.

"You like him, too, don't you?" observed Hugh.

She nodded.

"Then maybe you'll like what I brought you." He turned suddenly, ran out to his car, and came back with a squirming little ball of fur, which he thrust into her hands. "That," he said with a shy grin, "is Captain Kidd II. Son of Captain Kidd and Meriway."

Milly May stared at the pup with startled eyes which slowly turned starry. She had never seen a sweeter pup. His short button nose, his soft teddy-bear fur, and his bluish infant eyes were adorable. Son of Captain Kidd and Meriway! Bluest of blue blood. And he was hers!

"He'll get some of them at least," remarked Hugh, vaguely.

"Some of what?" asked Milly May.

"Ribbons," said Hugh with certainty.

* * * * *

"Captain Kidd's Ribbons," by Dee Dunsing. Published January 29, 1939, in *The Girl's Companion*. Reprinted by permission of Joe Wheeler (P. O. Box 1246, Conifer, Colorado 80433) and Cook Communications Ministries, Colorado Springs, Colorado. Dee Dunsing wrote for inspirational and popular magazines during the first half of the twentieth century.

Annie, the Railroad Dog

Phil Walker

A whole city in love with a dog? Hard to believe, but it was true. Some time ago, I was being interviewed by Phil Walker (award-winning broadcaster and writer, the voice of Fort Collins and the Poudre Valley for over forty years now) on Radio Station KCOL. I had just reduced him to tears with one of the most emotional stories in my latest anthology. But for the first time in all my years of being interviewed, I had the tables turned on me: Walker took the rest of our broadcast time reading this story—putting me out of commission!

* * * * *

This is a story about a dog—and a city's love affair with her. In the early 1930s, the twin colossuses of the Depression and the Great Dust Bowl stood astride a prostrate Colorado and had brought the city of Fort Collins to its knees. In the embattled homes, stores, and offices of the city, the lights burned around the clock as the dust storms marched across the plains, endlessly, blotting out the sun. There was no money, no jobs, no crops, no credit, and no end in sight. The two or three thousand families in town had a tendency to band together and focus on living a day at a time. Traditions ran deep.

The most modern transportation that people had was the railroad. Certainly there were a fair number of cars in town by this time, but there were no interstate highways, and cars were a local phenomenon. If you wanted to really get somewhere, you took the train. This meant that a lot of people went in and out of the main train station, and it was a popular meeting place.

In 1934, a train heading for Fort Collins steamed into the little town of Timnath, several miles to the east, on a cold winter morning. Across the street from the station was a blacksmith shop, and a couple of the railroad men happened to have business there.

"Hey, Frank! Come here a minute. Look what I found!"

Hiding in the back of the shop was a little collie, barely more than a puppy. She was cold and shivering and starving. However, she must have been a real personality because she charmed those tough old railroad guys right out of their bib overalls. Times were hard in 1934, and a stray dog just didn't attract a lot of attention amidst the general misery of the Poudre Valley. This one did.

"Cute little thing," said Frank, and he reached down and scooped the dog into his arms. The dog raised her nose toward his face and eked out a tiny, forlorn bark, followed by a slurpy, wet kiss.

"Awww," said the man, "you're a good girl!" He scratched her ears and smoothed her fur.

"Let's take her home with us," suggested the other man.

"I don't dare bring home another animal to feed," declared Frank. "My wife wouldn't allow it."

"She can live at the depot," said the other man. "She'll be our mascot."

So the railroad men took the little dog onto the train and brought her back to Fort Collins and gave her a home. They also gave her a name. They called her Annie. Annie lived at the depot on Laporte Street, just off College Avenue, and she turned out to be one of those rare personalities that charmed everybody.

From then on, Annie was a permanent fixture at the Fort Collins railroad depot—known and loved by the whole town. Whenever a train chugged into the station, Annie would faithfully march out to the platform and greet every passenger. Annie was the unofficial ambassador of the city, and newcomers were often amazed to see local people get off the train and run to greet the little dog before they would greet their own families! She never strayed very far from the station. It was her empire, and she was the reigning queen.

You see, Annie had come at the worst part of the Depression and the dust storms. She was a bright little light in otherwise drab and dreary days. People had come to think of her as a symbol of better times. She represented something permanent, reliable, and beautiful. The citizens of Fort Collins cherished her.

By 1941 things had begun to look up. Business was better, agriculture was improving, and the dust storms had come to an end. The future was bright. But the world outside had grown a little unlovely, and much of it was at war. When Pearl Harbor was bombed in December, the United States was drawn into World War II.

Very soon, young men from Fort Collins and the Poudre Valley started to leave for the military bases. The scenes were all the same: little clusters of friends and family would gather around a young man on the platform of the downtown train station and say their last tearful goodbyes. Almost always, just as the train was about to pull out of the station, the young man would reach down and give the faithful little collie a final pat and admonish her, "Annie, you be a good dog until I get back."

Annie would bark an encouraging farewell, and then the young man would be gone. Annie the railroad dog said goodbye to them all . . . some of them for the last time.

The years passed. By the end of 1945, the boys who had gone away to war now began returning to Fort Collins—older, wiser, and eager to get on with their lives. Every day, they could be seen staring anxiously through the windows of the trains as they pulled into the station in Fort Collins.

Once again the scenes of families, friends, and loved ones gathering around the soldiers and sailors were repeated, but now with a much happier outcome. And in the midst of all this, the faithful railroad collie, Annie, was there to bark a greeting and welcome home each favorite son. It was not at all uncommon to see tough, battle-weary veterans sink down on the station platform and take the little dog in their arms and cry, while Annie licked their faces and dried their tears. In those moments, each man knew that he was really home and that the war was truly over.

Now the exciting years of expansion and growth began. Prosperity brought an expanding population. New homes and businesses were built. Fort Collins was busy shaking off the ravages of all the terrible things they had been putting up with for so many years: dust storms, depressions, drought, war, rationing, and hoping somebody in your family didn't get killed. There was a great sense that the future potential for Fort Collins was nothing less than spectacular.

But there was one soul in town whose work was now finished and whose life was near its end.

Although railroad engines continued to chug into the station on Mason Street, just off Laporte Avenue, they came less often, and they pulled fewer passenger cars. Most people now were finding it more convenient to use their cars since the roads had been enlarged and improved. In Denver, they had even started to build a thing called a "freeway."

Nevertheless, the arrival of a train was always the signal for Annie to struggle to her feet and valiantly meet every passenger with a little "woof" and a wag of her tail. Her arthritis had gotten so much worse in the last couple of years that it was getting harder and harder for her to get around.

At last, the tough old railroaders just couldn't let her suffer any more. In her fourteenth year, she was put to sleep.

Fort Collins wept.

Annie had seen them all through the tough times. There had been times in the past when the only thing that seemed right about the city was that little dog. The men of the Colorado and Southern Railroad broke all the rules and buried her right next to the tracks where she had spent her life. And they also put up a three-foot-tall headstone that said, "From C and S Men, to Annie . . . Our Dog." Half the town showed up for the funeral.

The gravesite was destroyed some years later when the tracks were repositioned, but the gravestone is preserved today at the Fort Collins Museum where it can be seen and the story told over and over again.

It is the story of a dog—and a city—and a love affair that never ends.

* * * * *

"Annie, the Railroad Dog," by Phil Walker. Included in *Visions Along the Poudre Valley* (Fort Collins, Colo.: Phil Walker Communications, 1995). Reprinted by permission of the author. Phil Walker, award-winning broadcaster, was the radio voice of Fort Collins for many years. Today, with his Visions of the Platte series, he covers the entire state of Nebraska from radio station KFOR in Lincoln.

To Everything a Season

P. J. Platz

Maestro was getting old. But a chilling thought rose within Ruth: What if it were more than just that?

*   *   *   *   *

Ruth eased the pickup to a gentle stop in front of the squat brick building, then reached across the steering wheel with her left hand to turn off the key. Her right hand was fully occupied stroking the soft head cradled on her lap.

"Well Maestro, we're here," she said softly, running her hand back to the ruff of hair that bunched at his shoulders.

The German shepherd lifted his majestic head with an effort and fixed her with a liquid, trusting gaze.

"I know, boy; I know," she murmured, cradling the great head in both hands, bending to press her cheek against the dry nose. A massive tongue lashed her face weakly, and the tail thumped against the opposite door. "Come on, fellah. Let's get you healthy again."

She jumped down from the truck and held the door open for the dog, feeling her heart contract as she watched him jump heavily to the ground. He circled behind her legs, then sagged into a sitting position with his head precisely aligned with her left knee, waiting patiently. He would wait there forever, she knew, comfortably motionless until her own movement guided him forward. That was Tom's doing. "If we're going to have a big dog, Ruth, he's going to be perfectly trained." That had been Tom's standard answer whenever she complained about the long drive to obedience school or the endless sessions in the backyard with collar and leash. She smiled, remembering. He had been so proud of this dog.

"Good boy, Maestro," she praised him, knowing it was an effort for him to maintain such discipline, to remain sitting so rigidly when his body wanted to collapse. She closed the truck door quietly and walked toward the building, moving slowly so the old dog could keep up.

"I'm afraid you can't bring that dog in here without a leash," a stern-faced woman proclaimed from behind the counter in the vet's office.

"Maestro hasn't worn a collar or a leash since he was a puppy," Ruth said quietly. "Besides, on the phone the doctor said he would see him right away."

The woman peered over the counter and sniffed in irritation. Maestro raised his head politely to look at her, blinked once, then turned his nose pointedly away.

"Oh, the shepherd. Are you Ruth Brent?"

"Yes, I am."

The woman grunted in obvious disapproval at having her rules violated, then made a check mark on a clipboard. "The doctor is waiting for you." She jerked her head to the left, and Ruth moved toward the corridor. Maestro rose at the same instant her leg eased forward and shadowed her down the hall to the examination room.

"Come in. Ruth, isn't it? And . . ."

"Maestro. His name is Maestro."

The vet needed a haircut. Thick blond hair fell persistently over his eyes, and he kept pushing it back with impatient swipes of his hand.

Tom used to do that when his hair got too long. It always seemed to grow so fast. She would cut it one week, and by the next it was falling in his eyes again. Then she would get out the sewing scissors and make him sit in the old straight-backed wooden chair, and he would call her Delilah while she snicked away at the rich black curls.

She watched the vet push once again at a sweep of blond so unlike Tom's, fascinated by the gesture. He blushed under her scrutiny and grinned sheepishly.

"Sorry. I'm not usually this unkempt," he apologized. "Too busy to make time for a haircut."

She was embarrassed to have been caught staring and tried for a smile. It didn't quite make it to her lips as her eyes fell on the waist-high stainless steel table. "I don't think he can make it up there today," she said, her hand reaching automatically for Maestro's head. The dry nose tipped up to nuzzle her palm.

"He won't have to." The vet turned to a corner sink and began scrubbing his hands, continuing to talk over his shoulder. "I've read his records. According to Doc Hanson, our dog never needed anything but his annual shots. Looks like he's the healthiest patient I inherited when I bought this practice."

"I didn't know Doc Hanson was leaving," she said lamely, feeling somehow guilty for the ignorance.

"Retiring," he corrected.

He had nice eyes. Kind eyes, with those fine little lines at the edges that come from smiling a lot.

"I'm Dr. Walters, by the way. Nathaniel to my mother, Nate to everyone else. Nice to meet you."

He smiled briefly, then crouched directly in front of Maestro. "Hello, fellah. Nice to meet you, too."

Maestro stretched his neck to nose the proffered hand, and approved the scent and the man with a weak thump of his tail.

"He's ten, isn't he?" Nate looked up from his crouch, swiping at his hair again.

"He'll be eleven in three months."

The vet's hands ran over Maestro's body in gentle strokes that disguised a skillful examination. "That's a fine age for a shepherd, especially one in this condition. You've taken good care of him."

"We take good care of each other."

Nate pressed his hands against his knees and pushed himself to his feet, then laid one hand on top of Maestro's head as if he were blessing him—or passing a sentence. Maestro's tail swished back and forth on the linoleum floor. "He has a problem," he said quietly.

The words dropped from his mouth like so many pellets and seemed to resonate in the relative quiet of the room.

"How can you tell?" she asked weakly. "You barely touched him."

He brushed nervously at his hair and looked directly into her eyes. "There's a large mass here," he touched Maestro's side, "and another here, in the throat. I'll take X-rays, of course, and run the blood tests, but you should know now, it doesn't look good. Not at his age."

She stood absolutely still, saying nothing. She could hear the sharp yips of a small dog—a terrier, probably—coming from the kennels behind the building. For some reason it seemed very important to count the barks. She got all the way to twelve before he spoke again.

"Let's take some pictures," he said kindly. "Then we'll know more."

Ruth drove home slowly with Maestro's head resting on her lap, making a conscious effort not to notice the spring scenery sliding past her window. Was it only last week she had marveled at the vibrant shoots of green piercing the winter-dried meadows? The pink and white apple blossoms sprouting miraculously from the gnarled branches of near-naked trees? Such gaudy displays of new life seemed almost obscene now, when Maestro was dying.

"Stop it!" she hissed aloud, and Maestro raised his head in sudden attention at the sound of her voice. "He's only a dog," she chanted over and over, stroking the thick fur. "Only a dog."

She pulled into the long, curving drive, cautious of the deep ruts left by the spring rain, and eased the truck up to the big front porch of the massive old farmhouse. "We're home, boy," she whispered. Maestro pushed himself up to a sitting position, looked out the window, then opened his mouth in a doggy smile.

She kept herself busy for the rest of the day with a dozen mindless chores, staying as far from the phone as she could. Dr. Walters had promised to call after he finished the lab tests, and she knew already that she didn't want to hear the results.

Late in the afternoon she stabbed a sheet on the line with a nasty jab of a clothespin, fighting the wind in the flapping fabric as if it were a mortal enemy. *Funny,* she thought, *how you could just keep doing ordinary things, even when your world was collapsing around you.*

She remembered thinking the same thing when Tom died. Tom was gone, but still she had to eat, to pick up the mail, to take out the garbage, and none of it made any sense at all. Tom was dead, and the mailman still came. For a long time she hadn't been able to understand why the rest of the world hadn't stopped.

She'd been a little crazy then. No, she amended with a grim smile, she'd been a lot crazy. They'd been together five years, married since college, holding off on kids, socking every spare dime into renovating the old farmhouse. "Just us, for a while, Rudy." Tom had always called her Rudy instead of Ruth, as if one syllable hadn't been enough to say all he wanted to say when he spoke her name. "We'll get a good start to pass on to the kids when they come, and we'll have a long honeymoon to remember when we're old."

But they weren't destined to grow old together. Tom had died the year they finally finished the house, and every time she wondered why she hadn't been in the car with him that night, why she hadn't died too, the inane answer came to her: If they had both died, who would feed Maestro?

Sick, sick, sick, she screamed inside her head. *Other widows lived for their children; you lived for a stupid dog. You never even liked dogs much, not before Tom.*

The sting of hot tears prickled behind her eyes. She let two fall while she finished hanging the last sheet, then brushed angrily at her cheeks, and stomped back toward the house.

Maestro's single warning bark from inside the house announced a visitor just as she reached the door, and she turned to see a white pickup lumbering up the drive. She shaded her eyes with her hand and peered out across the yard, a little irritated at the intrusion, a little curious. She never had visitors anymore. Never. The town had learned long ago that her grief despised company.

Dr. Walters climbed down from the truck and walked toward her, one hand raised in silent greeting, his expression somber. "You didn't answer your phone," he said. "So I decided to stop in. Hope that's all right." He looked down at a dusty boot he scuffed back and forth across the old brick walk. "I've always wondered who lived here. I pass your place every morning on my way to the clinic." His eyes took in the sweep of lawn, the newly turned flower beds, the stately walnut trees shaking tight little buds in the breeze. "Beautiful spot."

"Thank you." Ruth barely managed to speak the words, and they hurt her throat on their way out. She jumped a little at another impatient bark from inside the house. "Come in, please. I'll make coffee."

He must miss Tom, Ruth thought later, watching Maestro wriggle closer to Nate's legs, laying the ultimate canine claim by planting his head across the vet's knees.

"There doesn't seem to be any pain," she said hesitantly, protesting what he wanted to do.

Nate shook his head with a strained smile, scratching absently behind Maestro's ear. "It's been with him a long time. Probably getting just a little worse every day. But soon, it will get a lot worse. All of a sudden. And then you'll know, but it will be too late to spare him."

She closed her eyes against the thought, but shook her head with a certainty she didn't feel. "I can't," she whispered. "I can't let you do it. Not yet."

"When?" he said so sharply that her eyes flew open in surprise. "When the pain is so bad that he can't take it anymore?"

She didn't understand his sudden harshness. He had been so kind, so understanding, just a moment ago. Now his face was stern, almost severe, with light brows lowered angrily over eyes that seemed to accuse her.

"You could let him go now, easily, before it gets unbearable. But you want to wait, don't you? You want to wait until there won't be any choice to make. Until he's hurting so bad you won't have any question about whether or not you're doing the right thing." He brushed his hair from his brow with a furious swipe of his hand. "Trouble is, Maestro will be the one who pays to make that decision easy for you. He'll have to go through hell to convince you it's time to let go."

She drew back in her chair in an effort to put more distance between them. "He was my husband's dog, too," she said shakily in some foolish, halfhearted attempt at defense, as if that statement alone would explain everything. He simply raised his brow in a silent question. "I'm a widow," she added in answer.

"For how long?"

What a strange thing for him to ask, she thought. *He's supposed to say something sympathetic. That's what people do when you tell them you're only half a person now. They tell you how sorry they are, how their thoughts are with you, that they're praying for you. She remembered with sudden, painful clarity how inexplicably angry that used to make her. The woeful faces, the standard lines, the empty sympathy from people who just couldn't understand.*

"Three years," she said flatly.

He brushed his hair away from his eyes again, and she felt a startling rush of anger. Why did he have to *do* that all the time?

"The Pearsons have a new litter of shepherds," he said abruptly. "First class. They'll be ready for homes next week."

"No! I don't want another dog. I won't try to replace Maestro. Not ever."

When he closed his eyes, he looked tired. A little exasperated, too, but mostly, just tired. She wondered what kind of hours he put in at the clinic.

"Will you have supper with me?" he asked after a moment. He must have seen something strange, something forbidden in her eyes, because he added quickly, "Nothing fancy. Just the Village Café."

"No," she said quickly, then tempered the refusal. "Thank you, no."

Oh, how she hated this. She had gone through it so many times, turning down the tentative offers from the area's eligible young men, all so foolish to think they could ease right in to where Tom had been, taking his place, making her forget.

"I don't date," she added firmly, deciding to cut this off before it could begin.

"But you do eat?"

"Of course I eat."

←————————————————————————————————→

"Good. If I ever decide to ask you for a date, I'll let you know. Right now, all I want is some supper, and I'm tired of eating alone. Let's go."

She spent the entire meal talking about Tom. She hadn't meant to, but he asked. The silly man asked what her husband had been like, and so she told him. And when she finished, he smiled a little. He only smiled little smiles, she noticed, never big ones, as if he found everything in the world quietly amusing. And then he said, "That's nice."

"What do you mean, 'That's nice'?" she asked, defensive and angry because those two words were such a small epitaph for Tom.

His smile broadened a little. "It's nice to hear about a good marriage for a change, that's all. No one ever seems to talk about those. All the things you said about Tom—well, they were nice. You must miss him very much."

There. He said something sympathetic, just like he was supposed to. But he had waited until he knew what she had was good before he said it. She felt the tears trying to come again, and chased them back inside.

Later he stopped the truck at her front door and waited for her to get out instead of walking her to the door. *Just like a friend,* she thought. *Not a date.*

"Thanks for supper," he said.

"You paid. I should thank you."

He chuckled a little. "You saved me from my own company. Tonight, I needed that."

She got out of the truck, then turned to lean back through the window. "I'm sorry I went on and on so much," she said lamely. *About Tom,* she added mentally.

"You shouldn't be. Sometimes it's good to remember."

She took a deep breath, nodded, then turned for the house.

"Ruth," he called after her. "You have to decide about Maestro."

"I know," she said without turning around. "I know."

He brought the puppy out the next day, a black-and-tan bundle of thick, soft fur wriggling constantly, falling down every few steps because its little tail wagged so hard, wet, pink tongue busily licking anything that got within range.

"I told you no," she said firmly, barely controlling the anger, staring down from the porch at the puppy's happy, innocent grin. She held her body rigid, all the more furious because Maestro seemed totally enamored of his tiny counterpart. He stood panting in the yard, his sides heaving with the effort of keeping track of the darting blur of youth. But whenever the pup came near, he swiped at it with his tongue, setting it back on its heels. It was a bitter contrast, seeing the puppy's vibrant health next to Maestro's fading energy.

Ruth bit down hard on her lower lip to keep from crying. *Everybody thought they had the answer. They all thought it was so easy. Lose something, lady? Get another. Husband, dog, whatever. There's plenty more where that one came from.*

"Get him out of here," she told Nate quietly. "Now."

Maestro sat in the driveway looking after the truck as it pulled away, his tail slowly brushing the dirt into an angel wing. He whined once, deep in his throat, then put his head down and walked slowly back to the shade of the porch. *He's stiffer today,* she thought.

Thirty minutes later the phone rang. Nate's voice was bright and casual, as if he had never been there a short time before, never noticed her anger. "Hi. I've thought about it, and I've decided. I'm calling to ask you for a date."

She almost laughed aloud. Chase the man off the place, and he calls to ask you out. "I don't date," she reminded him. "I told you that yesterday."

There was a short pause, then, "I forgot. OK. How about supper?"

"You bought me supper last night. I can't allow you to do it again." She was trying to be polite, but she meant it. If she accepted another meal from him, it would obligate her in some strange way.

"Great. You buy." He hung up before she could make a reply.

She stared into the phone's mouthpiece in disbelief, angry all over again because the man was too stubborn to take no for an answer. Worse yet, he hadn't even *let* her answer.

She spent the better part of the afternoon re-educating herself in the forgotten skill of cooking for two. She'd cooked, or rather not cooked, for one person for so long that even planning this meal seemed a task of inordinate difficulty. Not that she wanted to cook for him. It wasn't that at all. But she did owe him a meal, and she didn't want to encourage the town's wagging tongues by being seen in public with him again. So she'd feed him tonight, and that would be that. Even-steven. Paid in full.

She was purposefully careless, slamming down packages of frozen meat on the counter to thaw, examining the dwindling supply of vegetables in the freezer, then throwing them back in so hard that brittle beans cracked inside the plastic bags. "Vegetables, meat, salad!" she spat out the menu aloud, heard the hostility in her voice as it echoed in the empty kitchen, then slammed the freezer door shut and went out to the front porch.

The big wooden swing creaked pleasantly on its chains, soothing her with the monotony of its movement and its sound. She wondered idly how many miles she had put on this swing since Tom had hung it the year they moved in. "You can't have a front porch without a swing, Rudy," he'd told her. "It's against all the laws of nature. See? Even Maestro likes it." They'd both laughed when Maestro tried to climb up on the swing, balancing on his hind legs, looking at them in dismay when the strange moving chair wobbled and danced under the weight of his front paws. Since that day, his place had always been to the left of the swing, close enough so Tom's hand could hang over the edge, brushing the top of his head with every pass.

She looked down at where her fingers trailed over the thick fur, back and forth as the swing moved, and smiled at the dog. As if he could hear the smile, he lifted his head from his paws and looked up at her with that mute, expressive gaze more eloquent than a thousand human words. And then he whined.

He'd whined like that once before, the first night they spent alone in the house after Tom died. He'd trotted aimlessly from Tom's side of the bed to the window, then downstairs to the front door, then upstairs again to Ruth's side of the bed, whining the agonizing question, licking the salty tears from her face. She'd heard the regular clicks of his nails on the wooden floors for most of the night, then finally, she had patted Tom's side of the bed. He'd jumped up and laid down with a heavy, mournful sigh, his nose buried deep in Tom's pillow, sensing somehow that if he were allowed in his master's place, then his master wouldn't be coming back. The whining had stopped then, and Ruth had finally fallen asleep, her hand on Maestro's side, drawing comfort from the weight and warmth of another body on the big, empty bed.

Maestro's head lifted suddenly under her hand, and she blinked rapidly, coming back from the past. His throat rumbled, then he stood slowly, gaze riveted to the end of the drive, head lowered, shoulders hunched, ready as always to spring to her defense. The menacing posture altered immediately when the white truck turned into the drive, and Ruth shook her head sadly to see Maestro's tail lift in salute to the man who would be his executioner.

The old dog lumbered down the steps, his whine a melody now, singing an ecstatic greeting. Nate stooped to accept the effusive licks, rocking the big dog's head back and forth between his hands.

She watched the two communicate in that age-old, private language of man and dog, and was struck by the fanciful thought that she should have married again, if only for Maestro. A dog needed a man around.

Nate looked up and smiled a greeting, his hair hanging over his eyes. "Call me impulsive," he said sheepishly; "but I love this dog already. Even though I've only known him for two days, I'm hopelessly in love."

She grinned down at him and watched his little smile broaden into a big one. "He was depressed this morning after you left. I'm not sure whom he missed more—you or the puppy."

"Both, I hope. It would seem the pup and I come as a set." He tipped his head toward his truck, and Ruth saw ears flopping madly as the tiny form struggled to jump high enough to look out the open window.

"You kept him," she said quietly.

"I had to. Rejection is a terrible thing for a puppy. I was afraid he wouldn't get over it."

She chuckled and shook her head as Maestro walked stiffly over to the truck, his tail waving. "Better let him out. He'll keep Maestro company while you help with supper."

His brows lifted slightly. "We're having supper here? You're cooking for a man? That's perilously close to a date, isn't it?"

"Certainly not. You'll notice I didn't even change clothes," she gestured at her jeans and sweatshirt.

"Is that how you tell? If you change clothes, then it's a date?"

She nodded. "That's how you tell."

Nate helped Ruth as she set pots to simmer on the stove, then they went out to the porch swing. Maestro and the pup were lying side by side on the grass, panting in a syncopated chorus of happy exhaustion.

Ruth watched the two for a moment, then made herself ask the question, never taking her eyes off the dogs. "How long for Maestro? If he were yours, how long?"

Nate took a deep breath and let it out slowly. She could feel his eyes shift from her face, down to Maestro, then back to her again. She knew what he was going to say, and her stomach curled into knots as she waited to hear the words spoken. He'd say it should have been done days ago, or weeks ago, or now, maybe tonight, tomorrow morning. He'd put a time to the awful thing, and that would make it real.

"Soon."

"What?"

He cleared his throat, sighed again. "We'll watch him carefully. We won't let him suffer."

Now this is stupid, she thought, *blinking back the tears. You expected him to say you had to do it right away, and you could have listened to that dry-eyed. How silly that because he didn't say it, you can't stop crying.* "He's stiffer today," she said carefully, afraid to lend too much importance to the words.

"I know. It's a little worse. Just a little."

"Do you think he has much pain?"

He shifted his weight a bit, and her side of the swing jiggled. She stiffened instantly. It was the first time since Tom's death that the swing had moved under her without her pushing it.

"He has some," he answered, looking down at his hands. "But he seems content now. Look at him."

Maestro sensed that he was the object of their attention and waved the flag of his tail.

"Besides, life is worth a little pain. It's that good sometimes." He said it softly, hesitantly, not as a vet, not as a professional, but as a man who understood.

The pup pounced on Maestro's neck, little paws wrapped around the massive head, tiny teeth gnawing at the graying muzzle. Maestro just lay there, blinking languidly, clearly contemptuous of the youngster's childish behavior, but tolerating it nonetheless.

Nate cleared his throat and frowned, watching the dogs as he spoke. "I never meant for the pup to replace Maestro, you know. No dog will ever do that."

She turned and saw the concern in his eyes.

"But he's good for Maestro now." He spoke slowly, as if each word were a step on ground that threatened to crumble beneath him. "And he'll be good for you later." He took another deep breath. "Replacing something you love isn't erasing it. You've just got to have someplace new for the love to go. That's all."

She felt the smile touch her lips, and her eyes, and thought how strange it was that she didn't feel like crying anymore. Oh, she would. Tomorrow, the next day, maybe next week; whenever the time came she would cry and cry for Maestro. But not yet. Now it was enough to lean back against the swing, close her eyes, and rock to the push of someone else's foot.

She gave in to it, letting herself relax, vaguely aware of the sound of the dogs' panting, the busy chirps of sparrows settling in for the night, the gentle ordinary sounds of life.

Soon they would go in to supper. And afterward, she thought with a smile, afterward, if there were time, maybe she'd cut his hair.

* * * * *

"To Everything a Season," by P. J. Platz. Reprinted by permission of Tracy and Patricia Lambrecht. P. J. Platz is a successful mother/daughter writing team who live in Chisago City, Minnesota. They are prolific writers of short stories as well as movie scripts, and their work shows up in contemporary women's and family magazines.

Don

Zane Grey

In 1907, Buffalo Jones, the man who almost single-handedly saved the American buffalo from extinction by lassoing their calves, decided to lasso mountain lions on the rim of the Grand Canyon of the Colorado. Zane Grey, the frontier writer, was one of the party, as were a number of dogs Jones hoped would soon become lion dogs. Among these dogs was Don.

Zane Grey's story of Don was eventually published as a book. In time, it has come to be considered one of the greatest dog stories ever written.

* * * * *

It has taken me years to realize the greatness of a dog, and often as I have told the story of Don—his love of freedom and hatred of men, how I saved his life and how he saved mine—it never was told as I feel it now.

I saw Don first at Flagstaff, Arizona, where arrangements had been made for me to cross the desert with Buffalo Jones and a Mormon caravan en route to Lee's Ferry on the Colorado River. Jones had brought a pack of nondescript dogs. Our purpose was to cross the river and skirt the Vermilion Cliffs and finally work up through Buckskin Forest to the north rim of the Grand Canyon, where Jones expected to lasso mountain lions and capture them alive. The most important part of our outfit, of course, was the pack of hounds. Never had I seen such a motley assembly of canines. They did not even have names. Jones gave me the privilege of finding names for them.

Among them was a hound that seemed out of place because of his superb proportions, his sleek dark smooth skin, his noble head, and great solemn black eyes. He had extraordinarily long ears, thick-veined and faintly tinged with brown. Here was a dog that looked to me like a thoroughbred. My friendly overtures to him went unnoticed. Jones said he was part blood hound and had belonged to an old Mexican don in southern California. So I named him Don.

We were ten days crossing the Painted Desert, and protracted horseback riding was then so new and hard for me that I had no enthusiasm left to scrape acquaintance with the dogs. Still I did not forget and often felt sorry for them as they limped along, clinking their chains under the wagons. Even then I divined that horses and dogs were going to play a great part in my Western experience.

At Lee's Ferry we crossed the Colorado, and I was introduced to the weird and wild canyon country, with its golden-red walls and purple depths. Here we parted with the caravan and went on with Jones's rangers, Jim and Emmet, who led our outfit into such a wonderful region as I had never dreamed of. We camped several days on the vast range where Jones let his buffalo herd run wild. One day the Arizonians put me astride a white mustang that apparently delighted in carrying a tenderfoot. I did not then know what I was soon to learn—that the buffalo always chased this mustang off the range. When I rode up on the herd, to my utter amazement and terror they took after me and—but I am digressing, and this is a dog story.

Once across the river, Jones had unchained the dogs and let them run on ahead or lag behind. Most of them lagged. Don for one, however, did not get sore feet. Beyond the buffalo range we entered the sage, and here Jones began to train the dogs in earnest. He carried on his saddle an old blunderbuss of a shotgun, about which I had wondered curiously. I had supposed he meant to use it to shoot small game.

Moze, our black-and-white dog, and the ugliest of the lot, gave chase to a jack rabbit.

"Hyar, you Moze, come back!" bawled Jones in stentorian tones. But Moze paid no attention. Jones whipped out the old shotgun, and before I could utter a protest he had fired. The distance was pretty far—seventy yards or more—but Moze howled piercingly and came sneaking and limping back. It was remarkable to see him almost crawl to Jones's feet.

"Thar! That'll teach you not to chase rabbits. You're a lion dog!" shouted the old plainsman as if he were talking to a human.

At first I was so astounded and furious that I could not speak. But presently I voiced my feeling.

"Wal, it looks worse than it is," he said, with his keen gray-blue eyes on me. "I'm usin' fine birdshot, an' it can't do any more than sting. You see, I've no time to train these dogs. It's necessary to make them see quick that they're not to trail or chase any varmints but lions."

There was nothing for me to do but hold my tongue, though my resentment appeared to be shared by Jim and Emmet. They made excuses for the old plainsman. Jim said, "He shore can make animals do what he wants. But I never seen the dog or hoss that cared two bits for him."

We rode on through the beautiful purple-sage land, gradually uphill, toward a black-fringed horizon that was Buckskin Forest. Jack rabbits, cottontails, coyotes and foxes, prairie dogs, and pack rats infested the sage and engaged the attention of our assorted pack of hounds. All the dogs except Don fell victim to Jones' old blunderbuss, and surely stubborn Moze received a second peppering, this time at closer range. I espied drops of blood upon his dirty white skin. After this it relieved me greatly to see that not even Moze transgressed again. Jones's method was cruel, but effective. He had captured and subdued wild animals since his boyhood. In fact, that had been the driving passion of his life, but no sentiment entered into it.

"Reckon Don is too smart to let you ketch him," Jim once remarked to our leader.

"Wal, I don't know," responded Jones, dubiously. "Mebbe he just wouldn't chase this sage trash. But wait till we jump some deer. Then we'll see. He's got bloodhound in him, and I'll bet he'll run deer. All hounds will, even the best ones trained on bear an' lion."

Not long after we entered the wonderful pine forest the reckoning of Don came as Jones had predicted. Several deer bounded out of a thicket and crossed ahead of us, soon disappearing in the green blur.

"Ahuh! Now we'll see," Jones said deliberately pulling out the old shotgun.

The hounds trotted along beside our horses, unaware of the danger ahead. Soon we reached the deer tracks. All the hounds showed excitement. Don let out a sharp yelp and shot away like a streak on the trail.

"Don, come hyar!" yelled Jones, at the same time extending his gun. Don gave no sign he had heard. Then Jones pulled trigger and shot him. I saw the scattering of dust and pine needles all round Don. He doubled up and rolled. I feared he might be badly injured. But he got up and turned back. It seemed strange that he did not howl. Jones drew his plunging horse to a halt and bade us all stop.

"Don, come back hyar," he called in a loud, harsh, commanding voice.

The hound obeyed, not sneakingly or cringingly. He did not put his tail between his legs. But he was frightened and no doubt pretty badly hurt. When he reached us, I saw that he was trembling all over and that drops of blood dripped from his long ears. What a somber sullen gaze in his eyes!

"See hyar," bellowed Jones, "I knowed you was a deer chaser. Wal, now you're a lion dog."

Later that day, when I had recovered sufficiently from my disapproval, I took Jones to task about this matter of shooting the dogs. I wanted to know how he expected the hounds to learn what he required of them.

"Wal, that's easy," he replied curtly. "When we strike a lion trail I'll put them on it—let them go. They'll soon learn."

It seemed plausible, but I was so incensed that I doubted the hounds would chase anything, and I resolved that if Jones shot Don again, I would force the issue and end the hunt unless assured there would be no more of such drastic training methods.

Soon after this incident, we made camp on the edge of a beautiful glade where a snow bank still lingered and a stream of water trickled down into a green swale. Before we got camp pitched, a band of wild horses thudded by, thrilling me deeply. My first sight of wild horses! I knew I should never forget that splendid stallion, the leader, racing on under the trees, looking back at us over his shoulder.

At this camp I renewed my attempts to make friends with Don. He had been chained apart from the other dogs. He ate what I fetched him, but remained aloof. His dignity and distrust were such that I did not risk laying a hand on him then. But I resolved to win him if it were possible. His tragic eyes haunted me. There was a story in them I could not read. He always seemed to be looking afar. On this occasion I came to the conclusion that he hated Jones.

* * *

Buckskin Forest was well named. It appeared to be full of deer, the large black-tailed species known as mule deer. This species must be related to the elk. Their size and beauty, the way they watched with long ears erect and then bounded off as if on springs, never failed to thrill me with delight.

As we traveled on, the forest grew wilder and more beautiful. In the parklike glades a bleached white grass waved in the wind and bluebells smiled wanly. Wild horses outnumbered the deer, and that meant there were always some in sight. A large gray grouse flew up now and then, and the most striking of the forest creatures to fascinate me was a magnificent black squirrel, with a long bushy white tail, tufted ears, and a red stripe down its glossy sides.

We rode for several days through this enchanting wilderness, gradually ascending, and one afternoon we came abruptly to a break in the forest. It was the north rim of the Grand Canyon. My astounded gaze tried to grasp an appalling abyss of purple and gold and red, a chasm too terrible and beautiful to comprehend all at once. The effect of that moment must have been tremendous, for I have never recovered from it. To this day the thing that fascinates me most is to stand upon a great height—canyon wall or promontory or peak—and gaze down into the mysterious colorful depths.

Our destination was Powell's Plateau, an isolated cape jutting out into the canyon void. Jones showed it to me—a distant gold-rimmed black-fringed promontory, seemingly inaccessible and unscalable. The only trail leading to it was a wild-horse hunter's trail, seldom used, exceedingly dangerous. It took us two days over this canyon trail to reach the Saddle—a narrow strip of land dipping down from the Plateau and reaching up to the main rim. We camped under a vast looming golden wall, so wonderful that it kept me from sleeping. That night lions visited our camp. The hounds barked for hours. This was the first chance I had to hear Don. What a voice he had! Deep, ringing, wild, like the bay of a wolf!

Next morning we ascended the Saddle, from the notch of which I looked down into the chasm still asleep in purple shadows; then we climbed a narrow deer trail to the summit of the Plateau. Here indeed was the grand wild isolated spot of my dreams. Indeed, I was in an all-satisfying trance of adventure.

I wanted to make camp on the rim, but Jones laughed at me. We rode through the level stately forest of pines until we came to a ravine, on the north side of which lay a heavy bank of snow. This was very necessary, for there was no water on the Plateau. Jones rode off to scout while the rest of us pitched camp. Before we had completed our tasks, a troop of deer appeared across the ravine, and motionless they stood watching us. There were big and little deer, blue-gray in color, sleek and graceful, so tame that to me it seemed brutal to shoot at them.

Don was the only one of the dogs that espied the deer. He stood up to gaze hard at them, but he did not bark or show any desire to chase them. Yet there seemed to me to be a strange yearning light in his dark eyes. I had never failed to approach Don whenever opportunity afforded, to continue my overtures of friendship. But now, as always, Don turned away from me. He was cold and somber. I had never seen him wag his tail or whine eagerly, as was common with most hounds.

Jones returned to camp jubilant and excited, as far as it was possible for the old plainsman to be. He had found lion trails and lion tracks, and he predicted a great hunt for us.

* * *

The Plateau resembled, in shape, the ace of clubs. It was perhaps six miles long and three or four wide. The body of it was covered with a heavy growth of pine, and the capes that sloped somewhat toward the canyon were thick with sage and cedar. This lower part, with its numerous swales and ravines and gorges, all leading down into the jungle of splintered crags and thicketed slopes of the Grand Canyon, turned out to be a paradise for deer and lion.

We found many lion trails leading down from the cedared broken rim to the slopes of yellow and red. These slopes really constituted a big country, and finally led to the sheer perpendicular precipices, three thousand feet lower.

Deer were numerous and as tame as cattle on a range. They grazed with our horses. Herds of a dozen or more were common. Once we saw a very large band. Down in the sage and under the cedars and in ravines we found many remains of deer. Jones called these lion-kills. And he frankly stated that the number of deer killed yearly upon the Plateau would be incredible to anyone who had not seen the actual signs.

In two days we had three captive lions tied up to pine saplings near camp. They were two-year-olds. Don and I had treed the first lion; I had taken pictures of Jones lassoing him. I had jumped off a ledge into a cedar to escape another. I had helped Jones hold a third. I had scratches from lion claws on my chaps, and—but I keep forgetting that this is not a story about lions. Always before when I have told it I have slighted Don.

One night, a week or more after we had settled in camp, we sat round a blazing red fire and talked over the hunt of the day. We all had our part to tell. Jones and I had found where a lioness had jumped a deer. He showed me where the lioness had crouched upon a little brushy knoll, and how she had leaped thirty feet to the back of the deer. He showed me the tracks the deer had made—bounding, running, staggering with the lioness upon its back—and where, fully a hundred paces beyond, the big cat had downed its prey and killed it. There had been a fierce struggle. Then the lioness had dragged the carcass down the slope, through the sage, to the cedar tree where her four two-year-old cubs waited. All that we found of the deer were the ragged hide, some patches of hair, cracked bones, and two long ears. These were still warm.

Eventually we got the hounds on this trail and soon caught up with the lions. I found a craggy cliff under the rim and sat there watching and listening for hours. Jones rode to and fro above me and at last dismounted to go down to join the other men. The hounds treed one of the lions. How that wild canyon slope rang with barks and bays and yells! Jones tied up this lion. Then the hounds worked up the ragged slope towards me, much to my gratification and excitement. Somewhere near me the lions had taken to cedars or crags, and I strained my eyes searching for them.

At last I located a lion on top of an isolated crag right beneath me. The hounds, with Don and Ranger leading, had been on the right track. My lusty yells brought the men. Then the lion stood up—a long, slender, yellowish cat—and spat at me. Next it leaped off the crag, fully fifty feet to the slope below, and bounded down, taking the direction from which the men had come. The hounds gave chase, yelping and baying. Jones bawled at them, trying to call them off, for what reason I could not guess. But I was soon to learn. The dogs found the lion Jones had captured and left lying tied under a cedar, and they killed it, then took the trail of the other. They treed it far down in the rough jumble of rocks and cedars.

One by one we had ridden back to camp that night, tired out. Jim was the last in, and he told his story last. And what was my amazement and fright to learn that all the three hours I had sat upon the edge of the caverned wall, the lioness had crouched on a bench above me! Jim on his way up had seen her, and then located her tracks in the dust back of my position. When this fact burst upon me, I remembered how I had at first imagined I heard faint panting breaths near me somewhere. I had been too excited to trust my ears.

"Wal," said Jones, standing with the palms of his huge hands to the fire, "we had a poor day. If we had stuck to Don there'd have been a different story. I haven't trusted him. But now I reckon I'll have to. He'll make the greatest lion dog I ever had. Strikes me as strange, too, for I never guessed it was in him. He has faults, though. He's too fast. He outruns the other hounds, an' he's goin' to be killed because of that. Some day he'll beat the pack to a mean old tom lion or a lioness with cubs, an' he'll get his everlastin'. Another fault is, he doesn't bark often. That's bad, too. You can't stick to him. He's got a grand bay, shore, but he saves his breath. Don wants to run an' trail an' fight alone. He's got more nerve than any hound I ever trained. He's too good for his own sake—and it'll be his death."

Naturally I absorbed all that Buffalo Jones said about dogs, horses, lions, everything pertaining to the West, and I believed it as if it had been gospel. But I observed that the others, especially Jim, did not always agree with our chief in regard to the hounds. A little later, when Jones had left the fire, Jim spoke up with his slow Texas drawl, "Wal, what does he know aboot dawgs? I'll tell you right heah, if he hadn't shot Don we'd had the best hound thet ever put his nose to a track. Don is a wild strange hound, shore enough. Mebbe he's like a lone wolf. But it's plain he's been mistreated by men. An' Jones has just made him wuss."

Emmet inclined to Jim's point of view. And I respected this giant Mormon who was famous on the desert for his kindness to men and animals. His ranch at Lee's Ferry was overrun with dogs, cats, mustangs, burros, sheep, and tamed wild animals that he had rescued.

"Yes, Don hates Jones and, I reckon, all of us," said Emmet. "Don's not old, but he's too old to change. Still, you can never tell what kindness will do to animals. I'd like to take Don home with me and see. But Jones is right. That hound will be killed."

"Now I wonder why Don doesn't run off from us?" inquired Jim.

"Perhaps he thinks he'd get shot again," I ventured.

"If he ever runs away it'll not be here in the wilds," replied Emmet. "I take Don to be about as smart as any dog ever gets. And that's pretty close to human intelligence. People have to live lonely lives with dogs before they understand them. I reckon I understand Don. He's either loved one master once and lost him, or else he has always hated all men."

"Humph! That's shore an idee," responded Jim, dubiously. "Do you think a dog can feel like that?"

"Jim, I once saw a little Indian shepherd dog lie down on its master's grave and die," returned the Mormon, sonorously.

"Well, I'll be!" exclaimed Jim, in mild surprise.

* * *

One morning Jim galloped in, driving the horses pell-mell into camp. Any deviation from the Texan's usual leisurely manner of doing things always brought us up short with keen expectation.

"Saddle up," called Jim. "Shore thar's a chase on. I seen a big red lioness up heah. She must have come down out of the tree whar I hang my meat. Last night I had a haunch of venison. It's gone. . . . Say, she was a beauty. Red as a red fox."

In a very few moments we were mounted and riding up the ravine, with the eager hounds sniffing the air. Always overanxious in my excitement, I rode ahead of my comrades. The hounds trotted with me. The distance to Jim's meat tree was a short quarter of a mile. I knew well where it was and, as of course the lion trail would be fresh, I anticipated a fine opportunity to watch Don. The other hounds had come to regard him as their leader. When we neared the meat tree, which was a low-branched oak shaded by thick silver spruce, Don elevated his nose high in the air. He had caught a scent even at a distance. Jones had said more than once that Don had a wonderful nose. The other hounds, excited by Don, began to whine and yelp and run around with noses to the ground.

I had eyes only for Don. How instinct he was with life and fire! The hair on his neck stood up like bristles. Suddenly he let out a wild bark and bolted. He sped away from the pack and like a flash passed that oak tree, running with his head high. The hounds strung out after him, and soon the woods seemed full of a baying chorus.

My horse, Black Bolly, well knew the meaning of that medley and did not need to be urged. He broke into a run and swiftly carried me up out of the hollow and through a brown-aisled pine-scented strip of forest to the canyon.

I rode along the edge of one of the deep indentations on the main rim. The hounds were bawling right under me at the base of a low cliff. They had jumped the lioness. I could not see them, but that was not necessary. They were running fast towards the head of this cove, and I had hard work to hold Black Bolly to a safe gait along that rocky rim. Suddenly he shied, and then reared, so that I fell out of the saddle as much as I dismounted. But I held the bridle and then jerked my rifle from the saddle sheath. As I ran towards the rim, I heard the yells of the men coming up behind. At the same instant I was startled and halted by sight of something red and furry flashing up into a tree right in front of me. It was the red lioness. The dogs had chased her into a pine, the middle branches of which were on a level with the rim.

My skin went tight and cold, and my heart fluttered. The lioness looked enormous, but that was because she was so close. I could have touched her with a long fishing pole. I stood motionless for an instant, thrilling in every nerve, reveling in the beauty and wildness of that great cat. She did not see me. The hounds below engaged all her attention. But when I let out a yell, which I could not stifle, she jerked spasmodically to face me. Then I froze again. What a tigerish-yellow flash of eyes and fangs! She hissed. She could have sprung from the tree to the rim and upon me in two bounds. But she leaped to a ledge below the rim, glided along that and disappeared.

I ran ahead and with haste and violence clambered out upon a jutting point of the rim, from which I could command the situation. Jones and the others were riding and yelling back where I had left my horse. I called for them to come.

The hounds were baying along the base of the low cliff. No doubt they had seen the lioness leap out of the tree. My eyes roved everywhere. This cove was a shallow V-shaped gorge, a few hundred yards deep and as many across. Its slopes were steep with patches of brush and rock.

All at once my quick eye caught a glimpse of something moving up the opposite slope. It was a long red pantherish shape. The lioness! I yelled with all my might. She ran up the slope, and at the base of the low wall she turned to the right. At that moment Jones strode heavily over the rough loose rocks of the promontory toward me.

"Where's the cat?" he boomed, his gray eyes flashing. In a moment more I had pointed her out. "Ha! I see. . . . Don't like that place. The canyon boxes. She can't get out. She'll turn back."

The old hunter had been quick to grasp what had escaped me. The lioness could not find any break in the wall, and manifestly she would not go down into the gorge. She wheeled back along the base of this yellow cliff. There appeared to be a strip of bare clay or shale rock against which background her red shape stood out clearly. She glided along, slowing her pace, and she turned her gaze across the gorge.

Then Don's deep bay rang out from the slope to our left. He had struck the trail of the lioness. I saw him running down. He leaped in long bounds. The other hounds heard him and broke for the brushy slope. In a moment they had struck the scent of their quarry and given tongue.

As they started down, Don burst out of the willow thicket at the bottom of the gorge and bounded up the opposite slope. He was five-hundred yards ahead of the pack. He was swiftly climbing. He would run into the lioness.

Jones gripped my arm in his powerful hand.

"Look!" he shouted. "Look at that fool hound! . . . Runnin' uphill to get to that lioness. She won't run. She's cornered. She'll meet him. She'll kill him. . . . Shoot her! Shoot her!"

I scarcely needed Jones's command to stir me to save Don, but it was certain that the old plainsman's piercing voice made me tremble. I knelt and leveled my rifle. The lioness showed red against the gray—a fine target. She was gliding more and more slowly. She saw or heard Don. The gun sight wavered. I could not hold steady. But I had to hurry. My first bullet struck two yards below the beast, puffing the dust. She kept on. My second bullet hit behind her. Jones was yelling in my ear. I could see Don out of the tail of my eye. . . . Again I shot. Too high! But the lioness jumped and halted. She lashed with her tail. What a wild picture! I strained—clamped every muscle—and pulled the trigger. My bullet struck right under the lioness, scattering a great puff of dust and gravel in her face. She bounded ahead a few yards and up into a cedar tree. An instant later Don flashed over the bare spot where she had waited to kill him, and in another his deep bay rang out under the cedar.

"Treed!" yelled Jones, joyfully pounding me on the back with his huge fist. "You saved that fool dog's life. She'd have killed him shore. . . . Wal, the pack will be there pronto, an' all we've got to do is go over an' tie her up. But it was a close shave for Don."

That night in camp, Don was not in the least different from his usual somber self. He took no note of my proud proprietorship or my hovering near him while he ate the supper I provided, part of which came from my own plate. My interest and sympathy had augmented to love.

Don's attitude toward the captured and chained lions never ceased to be a source of delight and wonder to me. All the other hounds were upset by the presence of the big cats. Moze, Sounder, Tige, Ranger would have fought these collared lions. Not so Don! For him they had ceased to exist. He would walk within ten feet of a hissing lioness without the slightest sign of having seen or heard her. He never joined in the howling chorus of the dogs. He would go to sleep close to where the lions clanked their chains, clawed the trees, whined and spat and squalled.

* * *

Several days after that incident of the red lioness we had a long and severe chase through the brushy cedared forest on the left wing of the Plateau. I did well to keep the hounds within earshot. When I arrived at the end of that run, I was torn and blackened by the brush, wet with sweat, and hot as fire. Jones, lasso in hand, was walking round a large cedar under which the pack of hounds was clamoring. Jim and Emmet were seated on a rock, wiping their red faces.

"Wal, I'll rope him before he rests up," declared Jones.

"Wait till . . . I get . . . my breath," panted Emmet.

"We shore oozed along this mawnin'," drawled Jim.

Dismounting, I untied my camera from the saddle and then began to peer up into the bushy cedar.

"It's a tom lion," declared Jones. "Not very big, but he looks mean. I reckon he'll mess us up some."

"Haw! Haw!" shouted Jim, sarcastically. The old plainsman's imperturbability sometimes wore on our nerves.

I climbed a cedar next to the one in which the lion had taken refuge. From a topmost fork, swaying to and fro, I stood up to photograph our quarry. He was a good-sized animal, tawny in hue, rather gray of face, and a fierce-looking brute. As the distance between us was not far, my situation was as uncomfortable as thrilling. He snarled at me and spat viciously. I was about to abandon my swinging limb when the lion turned away from me to peer down through the branches.

Jones was climbing into the cedar. Low and deep the lion growled. Jones held in one hand a long pole with a small fork at the end, upon which hung the noose of his lasso. Presently he got far enough up to reach the lion. Usually he climbed close enough to throw the rope, but evidently he regarded this beast as dangerous. He tried to slip the noose over the head of the lion. One sweep of the big paw sent pole and noose flying. Patiently Jones made ready and tried again, with similar result. Many times he tried. His patience and perseverance seemed incredible. One attribute of his great power to capture and train wild animals here asserted itself. Finally the lion grew careless or tired, at which instant Jones slipped the noose over its head.

Drawing the lasso tight, he threw his end over a thick branch and let it trail down to the men below. "Wait now!" he yelled and quickly backed down out of the cedar. The hounds were leaping eagerly.

"Pull him off that fork an' let him down easy so I can rope one of his paws."

It turned out, however, that the lion was hard to dislodge. I could see his muscles ridge and bulge. Dead branches cracked, the treetop waved. Jones began to roar in anger. The men replied with strained, hoarse voices. I saw the lion drawn from his perch and, clawing the branches, springing convulsively, he disappeared from my sight.

Then followed a crash. The branch over which Jones was lowering the beast had broken. Wild yells greeted my startled ears and a perfect din of yelps and howls. Pandemonium had broken loose down there. I fell more than I descended from that tree.

As I bounded erect, I espied the men scrambling out of the way of a huge furry wheel. Ten hounds and one lion comprised that brown whirling ball. Suddenly out of it a dog came hurtling. He rolled to my feet, staggered up.

It was Don. Blood was streaming from him. Swiftly I dragged him aside, out of harm's way. And I forgot the fight. My hands came away from Don wet and dripping with hot blood. It shocked me. Then I saw that his throat had been terribly torn. I assumed his jugular vein had been severed. Don lay down and stretched out. He looked at me with those great somber eyes. Never would I forget! He was going to die right there before my eyes.

"Oh, Don! Don! What can I do?" I cried in horror.

As I sank beside Don, one of my hands came in contact with snow. It had snowed that morning, and there were still white patches in shady places. Like a flash I ripped off my scarf and bound it round Don's neck. Then I scraped up a double handful of snow and placed that in my bandana handkerchief. This also I bound tightly round his neck. I could do no more. My hope left me then, and I had not the courage to sit there beside him until he died.

All the while I had been aware of a bedlam near at hand. When I looked, I saw a spectacle for a hunter. Jones, yelling at the top of his stentorian voice, seized one hound after the other by the hind legs and, jerking him from the lion, threw him down the steep slope. Jim and Emmet were trying to help while at the same time they avoided close quarters with that threshing beast. At last they got the dogs off and the lion stretched out. Jones got up, shaking his shaggy head. Then he espied me, and his hard face took on a look of alarm.

"Hyar . . . you're all . . . bloody," he panted plaintively, as if I had been exceedingly remiss.

Whereupon I told him briefly about Don. Then Jim and Emmet approached, and we all stood looking down on the quiet dog and the patch of bloody snow.

"Wal, I reckon he's a goner," said Jones, breathing hard. "Shore I knew he'd get his everlastin'."

"Looks powerful like the lion has aboot got his, too," added Jim.

Emmet knelt by Don and examined the bandage round his neck. "Bleeding yet," he muttered, thoughtfully. "You did all that was possible. Too bad! . . . The kindest thing we can do is to leave him here."

I did not question this, but I hated to consent. Still, to move him would bring on only more hemorrhage, and to put him out of his agony would have been impossible for me. Moreover, while there was life there was hope! Scraping up a goodly ball of snow, I rolled it close to Don so that he could lick it if he chose. Then I turned aside and could not look again. But I knew that tomorrow, or the following day, I would find my way back to this wild spot.

The accident to Don and what seemed the inevitable issue weighed heavily upon my mind. Don's eyes haunted me. I very much feared that the hunt had reached an unhappy ending for me. Next day the weather was threatening and, as the hounds were pretty tired, we rested in camp, devoting ourselves to needful tasks. A hundred times I thought of Don, alone out there in the wild breaks. Perhaps merciful death had relieved him of suffering. I would surely find out on the morrow.

But next day the indefatigable Jones desired to hunt in another direction, and, as I was by no means sure I could find the place where Don had been left, I had to defer that trip. We had a thrilling hazardous luckless chase, and I for one gave up before it ended.

Weary and dejected, I rode back. I could not get Don off my conscience. The pleasant woodland camp did not seem the same place. For the first time the hissing, spitting, chain-clinking, tail-lashing lions caused me irritation and resentment. I would have none of them. What was the capture of a lot of spiteful vicious cats to the life of a noble dog? Slipping my saddle off, I turned Black Bolly loose.

Then I imagined I saw a beautiful black long-eared hound enter the glade. I rubbed my eyes. Indeed there was a dog coming. "Don!" I shouted my joy and awe. Running like a boy, I knelt by him, saying I knew not what. Don wagged his tail! He licked my hand! These actions seemed as marvelous as his return. He looked sick and weak, but he was all right.

The handkerchief was gone from his neck, but the scarf remained, and it was stuck tight where his throat had been lacerated.

Later Emmet examined Don and said we had made a mistake about the jugular vein being severed. Don's injury had been serious, however, and without the prompt aid I had so fortunately given he would soon have bled to death. Jones shook his gray old locks and said, "Reckon Don's time hadn't come. Hope that will teach him sense." In a couple of days Don had recovered, and on the next he was back leading the pack.

A subtle change had come over Don in his relation to me. I did not grasp it so clearly then. Thought and memory afterward brought the realization to me. But there was a light in his eyes for me which had never been there before.

One day Jones and I treed three lions. The largest leaped and ran down into the canyon. The hounds followed. Jones strode after them, leaving me alone with nothing but a camera to keep those two lions up that tree. I had left horse and gun far up the slope. I protested; I yelled after him, "What'll I do if they start down?"

He turned to gaze up at me. His grim face flashed in the sunlight.

"Grab a club an' chase them back," he replied.

Then I was left alone with two ferocious-looking lions in a piñon tree scarcely thirty feet high. While they heard the baying of the hounds they paid no attention to me, but after that ceased they got ugly. Then I hid behind a bush and barked like a dog. It worked beautifully. The lions grew quiet. I barked and yelped and bayed until I lost my voice. Then they got ugly again! They started down. With stones and clubs I kept them up there, while all the time I was nearing to collapse. When at last I was about to give up in terror and despair, I heard Don's bay, faint and far away. The lions had heard it before I had. How they strained! I could see the beating of their hearts through their lean sides. My own heart leaped. Don's bay floated up, wild and mournful. He was coming. Jones had put him on the back trail of the lion that had leaped from the tree.

Deeper and clearer came the bays. How strange that Don should vary from his habit of seldom baying! There was something uncanny in this change. Soon I saw him far down the rocky slope. He was climbing fast. It seemed I had long to wait, yet my fear left me. On and up he came, ringing out that wild bay. It must have curdled the blood of those palpitating lions. It seemed the herald of that bawling pack of hounds.

Don espied me before he reached the piñon in which were the lions. He bounded right past it and up to me with the wildest demeanor. He leaped up and placed his forepaws on my breast. And as I leaned down, excited and amazed, he licked my face. Then he whirled back to the tree, where he stood up and fiercely bayed the lions. While I sank down to rest, overcome, the familiar baying chorus of the hounds floated up from below. As usual they were far behind the fleet Don, but they were coming.

* * *

Another day I found myself alone on the edge of a huge cove that opened down into the main canyon. We were always getting lost from one another. And so were the hounds. There were so many lion trails that the pack would split, some going one way, some another, until it appeared each dog finally had a lion to himself.

It was a glorious day. From far below, faint and soft, came the strange roar of the Rio Colorado. I could see it winding, somber and red, through the sinister chasm. Adventure ceased to exist for me. I was gripped by the grandeur and loveliness, the desolation and loneliness of the supreme spectacle of nature.

Then as I sat there, absorbed and chained, the spell of enchantment was broken by Don. He had come to me. His mouth was covered with froth. I knew what that meant. Rising, I got my canteen from the saddle and poured water into the crown of my sombrero. Don lapped it. As he drank so thirstily I noticed a bloody scratch on his nose.

"Aha! A lion has batted you one, this very morning," I cried. "Don . . . I fear for you."

He rested while I once more was lost in contemplation of the glory of the canyon. What significant hours these on the lonely heights! But then I only saw and felt.

Presently I mounted my horse and headed for camp, with Don trotting behind. When we reached the notch of the cove, the hound let out his deep bay and bounded down a break in the low wall. I dismounted and called. Only another deep bay answered me. Don had scented a lion or crossed one's trail. Suddenly several sharp deep yelps came from below, a crashing of brush, a rattling of stones. Don had jumped another lion.

Quickly I threw off sombrero and coat and chaps. I retained my left glove. Then, with camera over my shoulder and revolver in my belt, I plunged down the break in the crag. My boots were heavy soled and studded with hobnails. The weeks on these rocky slopes had trained me to fleetness and sure-footedness. I plunged down the sliding slant of weathered stone, crashed through the brush, dodged under the cedars, leaped from boulder to ledge and down from ledge to bench. Reaching a dry stream bed, I saw in the sand the tracks of a big lion and beside them smaller tracks that were Don's. And as I ran I yelled at the top of my lungs, hoping to help Don tree the lion. What I was afraid of was that the beast might wait for Don and kill him.

Such strenuous exertion required a moment's rest now and then, during which I listened for Don. Twice I heard his bay, and the last one sounded as if he had treed the lion. Again I took to my plunging, jumping, sliding descent; and I was not long in reaching the bottom of that gorge. Ear and eye had guided me unerringly for I came to an open place near the main jump-off into the canyon, and here I saw a tawny shape in a cedar tree. It belonged to a big tom lion. He swayed the branch and leaped to a ledge, and from that down to another, and then vanished round a corner of wall.

Don could not follow down those high steps. Neither could I. We worked along the ledge, under cedars, and over huge slabs of rock toward the corner where our quarry had disappeared. We were close to the great abyss. I could almost feel it. Then the glaring light of a void struck my eyes like some tangible thing.

At last I worked out from the shade of rocks and trees and, turning the abrupt jut of wall, I found a few feet of stone ledge between me and the appalling chasm. How blue, how fathomless! Despite my pursuit of a lion, I was suddenly shocked into awe and fear.

Then Don returned to me. The hair on his neck was bristling. He had come from the right, from round the corner of wall where the ledge ran, and where surely the lion had gone. My blood was up, and I meant to track that beast to his lair, photograph him if possible, and kill him. So I strode on to the ledge and round the point of wall. Soon I espied huge cat tracks in the dust, close to the base. A well-defined lion trail showed there. And ahead I saw the ledge—widening somewhat and far from level—stretch before me to another corner.

Don acted strangely. He followed me, close at my heels. He whined. He growled. I did not stop to think then what he wanted to do. But it must have been that he wanted to go back. But the heat of youth and the wildness of adventure had gripped me, and fear and caution were not in me.

Nevertheless my sensibilities were remarkably acute. When Don got in front of me there was something that compelled me to go slowly. Soon, in any event, I should have been forced to that. The ledge narrowed. Then it widened again to a large bench with cavernous walls overhanging it. I passed this safe zone to turn onto a narrowing ledge of rock that disappeared round another corner. When I came to this point I must have been possessed, for I flattened myself against the wall and worked round it.

Again the way appeared easier. But what made Don go so cautiously? I heard his growls; still, no longer did I look at him. I felt this pursuit was nearing an end. At the next turn I halted short, suddenly quivering. The ledge ended—and there lay the lion, licking a bloody paw.

Tumultuous indeed were my emotions, yet on that instant I did not seem conscious of fear. Jones had told me never, in close quarters, to take my eyes off a lion. I forgot. In the wild excitement of a chance for an incomparable picture, I forgot. A few precious seconds were wasted over the attempt to focus my camera.

Then I heard quick thuds. Don growled. With a start I jerked up to see the lion had leaped or run half the distance between us. He was coming. His eyes blazed purple fire. They seemed to paralyze me, yet I began to back along the ledge. Whipping out my revolver, I tried to aim. But my nerves had undergone such a shock that I could not aim. The gun wobbled. I dared not risk shooting. If I wounded the lion, it was certain he would knock me off that narrow ledge.

So I kept on backing, step by step. Don did likewise. He stayed between me and the lion. Therein lay the greatness of that hound. How easily he could have dodged by me to escape along the ledge! But he did not do it.

A precious opportunity presented when I reached the widest part of the bench. Here I had a chance, and I recognized it. Then, when the overhanging wall bumped my shoulder, I realized too late. I had come to the narrowing part of the ledge. Not reason but fright kept me from turning to run. Perhaps that might have been the best way out of the predicament. I backed along the strip of stone that was only a foot wide. A few more blind steps meant death. My nerve was gone. Collapse seemed inevitable. I had a camera in one hand and a revolver in the other.

That purple-eyed beast did not halt. My distorted imagination gave him a thousand shapes and actions. Bitter despairing thoughts flashed through my mind. Jones had said mountain lions were cowards, but not when cornered—never when there was no avenue of escape!

Then Don's haunches backed into my knees. I dared not look down but I felt the hound against me. He was shaking, yet he snarled fiercely. The feel of Don there, the sense of his courage, caused my cold thick blood to burst into hot gushes. In another second he would be pawed off the ledge or he would grapple with this hissing lion. That meant destruction for both, for they would roll off the ledge.

I had to save Don. That mounting thought was my salvation. Physically, he could not have saved me or himself, but this grand spirit somehow pierced to my manhood.

Leaning against the wall, I lifted the revolver and steadied my arm with my left hand, which still held the camera. I aimed between the purple eyes. That second was an eternity. The gun crashed. The blaze of one of those terrible eyes went out.

Up leaped the lion, beating the wall with heavy thudding paws. Then he seemed to propel himself outward, off the ledge into space—a tawny spread figure that careened majestically over and over, down . . . down . . . down to vanish in the blue depths.

Don whined. I stared at the abyss, slowly becoming unlocked from the grip of terror. I staggered a few steps forward to a wider part of the ledge, and there I sank down, unable to stand longer. Don crept to me, put his head in my lap.

I listened. I strained my ears. How endlessly long seemed that lion in falling! But all was magnified. At last puffed up a sliding roar, swelling and dying until again the terrific silence of the canyon enfolded me.

Presently Don sat up and gazed into the depths. How strange to see him peer down! Then he turned his sleek dark head to look at me. What did I see through the somber sadness of his eyes? He whined and licked my hand. It seemed to me Don and I were more than man and dog. He moved away then round the narrow ledge, and I had to summon energy to follow. Suddenly, I turned my back on that awful chasm and held my breath while I slipped round the perilous place. Don waited there for me, then trotted on. Not until I had gotten safely off that ledge did I draw a full breath. Then I toiled up the steep rough slope to the rim. Don was waiting beside my horse. Between us we drank the rest of the water in my canteen, and when we reached camp night had fallen. A bright fire and a good supper broke the gloom of my mind. My story held those rugged Westerners spellbound. Don stayed close to me, followed me of his own accord, and slept beside me in my tent.

* * *

Don

There came a frosty morning when the sun rose red over the ramparts of colored rock. We had a lion running before the misty shadows dispersed from the canyon depths.

The hounds chased him through the sage and cedar into the wild breaks of the north wing of the Plateau. This lion must have been a mean old tom, for he did not soon go down the slopes.

The particular section in which he at last took refuge was impassable for man. The hounds gave him a grueling chase, then one by one they crawled up, sore and thirsty. All but Don! He did not come. Jones rolled out his mighty voice, which pealed back in mocking hollow echoes. Don did not come. At noonday Jones and the men left for camp with the hounds.

I remained. I had a vigil there on the lofty rim, alone, where I could peer down the yellow-green slope and beyond to the sinister depths. It was a still day. The silence was overpowering. When Don's haunting bay floated up it shocked me. At long intervals I heard it, fainter and fainter. Then no more!

Still I waited and watched and listened. Afternoon waned. My horse neighed piercingly from the cedars. The sinking sun began to fire the Pink Cliffs of Utah and then the hundred miles of immense chasm over which my charmed gaze held dominion. How lonely, how terrifying that stupendous rent in the earth! Lion and hound had no fear. But thinking, feeling man was afraid. What did they mean—this exquisitely hued and monstrous canyon—the setting sun—the wildness of a lion, the grand spirit of a dog—and the wondering sadness of a man?

I rode home without Don. Half the night I lay awake waiting, hoping. But he did not return by dawn, nor through the day. He never came back.

* * * * *

"Don, the Story of a Lion Dog," by Zane Grey. Reprinted by permission of Loren Grey. Zane Grey (1872–1939), was born in Zanesville, Ohio. He was the highest-selling and highest-paid author in the world during the first half of the twentieth century. He is considered to be the "Father of the Western Novel," and the last chronicler of the frontier (while the frontier still existed). He was also one of the leading nature writers of his time.

Author Biographical Information
& Acknowledgements

Joe L. Wheeler, Ph.D., is the editor/compiler of the popular *Christmas in My Heart* books. Dubbed "America's Keeper of the Story" by Focus on the Family's James Dobson, Wheeler has also served as editor/compiler of the *Great Stories Remembered*, *Heart to Heart*, and *Forged in the Fire* collections. Dr. Wheeler is professor emeritus of English at Columbia Union College in Takoma Park, Maryland, and founder and executive director of Zane Grey's West Society. He and his wife, Connie, reside in Conifer, Colorado.

"Only the Dog" (Introduction) by Joseph Leininger Wheeler and Albert Payson Terhune. Copyright © 2004. Printed by permission of the author.

"Owney, the Post Office Dog," by Joseph Leininger Wheeler. Copyright © 2004. Printed by permission of the author.